IN THE DRIVING SEAT

JACKIE STEWART
at the wheel of his
World Championship winning Tyrrell Ford
Painting by Senga Murray

BY JACK WEBSTER

PUBLISHED BY

FOREWORD BY LORD MONTAGU OF BEAULIEU

COVER PAINTINGS BY SENGA MURRAY

THE GLASGOW ROYAL CONCERT HALL

The copyright © for the articles in this book belongs to Jack Webster
Cover paintings, © Senga Murray;
All other material © The Glasgow Royal Concert Hall

The publishers and the author gratefully acknowledge the invaluable assistance given by Ian Gordon and Nigel Kennedy.

Acknowledgements and photographs:
Ian Gordon (Mitchell Library), Nigel Kennedy, Brian Lambie (Albion Archive, Biggar), Cordelia Oliver, Chris George (Walter Alexander Ltd), Gavin Booth, Lynn McMurdo (Volvo Irvine), Diane Blackwood-Murray, Mike Ward (Grampian Transport Museum), Jack Asher (Doune Motor Museum), Donald & Sandra Cameron, Brian Heath (The Automobile), Betty Craig, Michael Mutch (Myreton Motor Museum), Winnie Tyrrell (Glasgow Museums), Alastair Smith (Museum of Transport, Glasgow), Graham Gauld, Elaine Catton-Quinn & Dan Wright (Albion Automotive), Robert Grieves, Tony Murray (The Herald), Wendy Jones, James Savage, Hamish MacLean, David Heathcote (Vintage Bus Museum), Stan Sproat, Bob Whitehill (Thomson Print Services), Sasha Pearl, Robert Stormont (Illinois, USA), Elaine Farrell (Press Office, AA), Sheila Callum, Ian Gray (Penman Engineering, Dumfries), Nicola Barr, Chris Rock, Tom Glen, Derek Butcher (Knockhill Racing Circuit), Alan Glen (TGRCH), Jonathan Lord (RSAC), Chris Christodoulou, Scott Ashforth (Marketing Dept, Arnold Clark Ltd), Yvette Le Couvey (Channel Islands), Tim Wright (Autosport), Nan & John Lindsay (Lindsay of Dumbuck), David Clark (SMTA), Edward Smith & John Napier (J McGavigan Automotive), Ross Finlay (The Herald), W K Henderson, J Thomson (Berwickshire Museum Services), Sybil Cavanagh (Bathgate Library), Alan Carlaw, Lawrence Gustin (Buick Motor Division, General Motors Michigan USA), Sandy and Logan Morrison (Morrison's of Stirling), Dr & Mrs S S I Parker, Mr & Mrs J W McInnes, R M Grant (Park Automobile), Strathclyde Regional Archives

Although every effort has been made to clear copyright, in some cases it has been difficult to trace holders. The publishers apologise for any omissions.

First published in Great Britain in 1996 by
THE GLASGOW ROYAL CONCERT HALL
2 Sauchiehall Street
Glasgow G2 3NY

ISBN 0 9522174 5 7

A catalogue record for this book is available from the British Library

Design, typesetting, and production
by Alan Carlaw, Giffnock, Glasgow
Printed by Elpeeko Ltd, Lincoln

Contents

	Introduction	55	Motor Sport
3	Contents	63	The Triumphs of Ecurie Ecosse
4	Foreword	66	Scotland's Stars of Motor Sport
6	Author's note	79	The Scottish Motor Trade
7	Preface	85	The Royal Scottish Automobile Club
8	The Argyll - A Leader in Europe	91	Scottish Motor Museums
18	Arrol-Johnston – The Mo-Car Men	95	MacBrayne for the Highlands
24	Albion – Sure as the Sunrise	97	Motoring Motivators
32	Motor Car Fever	98	Doonhamer Designers
38	The Great Pioneers	99	The Car with One Door
44	Model 'T' conquers Ben Nevis	100	Monte Carlo or Bust!
46	Rootes at Linwood	101	The Scots–American Connection
48	The Rise and Fall of Bathgate	103	Oliver & Sword - Collectors Supreme
50	Halley's Triumph	104	Motoring Miscellany
51	Alexanders Buses to Stagecoach	108	Scottish Registrations
54	Volvo at Irvine		About the Author

The inventor George Johnston designed the first commercial motor car to be produced in Glasgow. Called the Mo-Car, it was produced in 1896 and backed by some of Glasgow's most efficient businessmen, including Sir William Arrol and one of the Coats family. Wylie and Lochhead supplied the mahogany and solid oak needed for the body and the 'dogcart' design was powered by a Daimler engine.

Cover paintings by Senga Murray
Front cover – Argyll Motor Works, Alexandria
Rear cover – Arrol-Johnston lorry and Albion bus at Scotstoun
Subjects, material and photographic content selected by A B Carlaw, K P Colville, I Gordon & N A Kennedy

Foreword

by
Lord Montagu of Beaulieu

It has been observed that Scotland's major exports are brains and whisky. Comparatively few Scots seek to extract a living from their own country and it has always surprised me that so many of them sought to make cars there. In fact, it is one hundred years since the first petrol car ran on the roads of Scotland, though there were steam carriages north of the border before that, most famously the three-wheeled "road steamers" built in the late 1860s by R W Thompson of Edinburgh. In the mid-1840s, the ingenious Thompson had invented the pneumatic tyre but failed to make a commercial success of his "Aerial Wheels", leaving the long-forgotten idea to be reinvented by John Boyd Dunlop forty years later.

Self-propelled vehicles had been made in Scotland as early as 1827, when James Napier attempted to establish a fare-paying passenger service between Holy Loch and Loch Eck but was defeated by the poor state of the roads. In 1833, John Scott Russell built six steam coaches in the Grove House Works in Edinburgh and briefly ran a regular service from Glasgow to Paisley. One of Scott Russell's coaches had the melancholy distinction of being the cause of Scotland's first motoring fatality, when it burst its boiler when trying to get through a pile of stones laid across the road and killed several of its passengers.

When the petrol age dawned in the 1890s, the infant motoring press recorded that Scotland's first "independent autocar user" was T R B Elliot of Kelso, who took delivery of a 31/2hp Panhard & Levassor at the very end of 1895. By March 1896 he had already covered 200 miles - and been fined sixpence "for taking the road without a flagman going ahead".

Already the first steps towards a Scottish motor industry had been taken: when his experimental steam tramcar went up in flames in 1894, locomotive engineer George Johnston decided to investigate internal combustion and is reputed to have bought a German Daimler later that year. Next he bought a Panhard & Levassor and in 1897, in partnership with the architect of the Forth Bridge, Sir William Arrol, formed the Mo-Car Syndicate and began developing a uniquely Scottish motor car.

In the meantime an old-established Scottish coachbuilder, John Stirling of Hamilton, Lanarkshire, had unveiled what was claimed as "the first Scottish autocar" in January 1897. Only its varnished walnut carriage body had actually been built in Hamilton, however; its chassis had been supplied by Daimler of Coventry, whose incorporation on 14 January 1896 marked the official start of the British motor industry, and the engine had been built by Panhard & Levassor in

Paris. Stirling built Daimler-based cars and subsequently a rear-engined Panhard design in Glasgow until 1902, but a move that year to a factory near Edinburgh, built four years previously by Scotland's Astronomer Royal for an unsuccessful electric car venture, precipitated the end of Stirling car production in 1903.

The first Arrol Johnston "Mo-Car" had appeared during 1897, built at Camlachie in Glasgow. Powered by an idiosyncratic opposed-twin engine with four pistons, started by pulling on a rope through the floorboards, the Mo-Car was a lumbering dog-cart with three rows of seats, one row ahead of the driver and one behind, seated with their backs to him. It may have looked archaic even when it was new, but the Arrol-Johnston dog-cart remained in production until 1906. Production had moved to the Coats thread mills in Paisley after the Camlachie factory had burnt down in 1901.

By then, Arrol-Johnston had a rival. Two of its executives had broken away in 1899 to form the Glasgow-based Albion Motor Company, which also built varnished wood dog-carts, albeit more mechanically conventional. While Albion did build conventional cars between 1906 and 1913, the bulk of their business relied on the country house trade, and only shooting brakes and commercial vehicles were available after 1913. With their slogan "sure as the sunrise", Albion commercial vehicles were renowned long after the marque's absorption by Leyland in 1951.

The third of the "Three 'A's of Scotland" was Argyll, founded in 1899 by Alex Govan, who in 1900 unveiled a neat little shaft-driven car which was to all intents and purposes a copy of the contemporary Renault, with just enough difference not to provoke a lawsuit for infringement. Argyll soon progressed to building its own designs, which proved so popular that by 1904 the company had become Britain's biggest manufacturers. In 1905 Argyll built a grandiose terra-cotta factory near Loch Lomond, which my father officially opened in June 1906, but this amazing building, with its three gilded domes and lavish interior, was fated never to be used to capacity.

Meanwhile, Arrol-Johnston had abandoned the old dog-cart for more conventional cars designed by their new chief engineer J S Napier and with the personal backing of Sir William Beardmore, whose company later built cars and taxis under its own name. In 1905 Napier drove a horizontal-twin car into first place in the Isle of Man Tourist Trophy at an average of 34 mph, while in 1907 my father was consulted on the design of a special air-cooled car fitted with skis which Lieutenant Ernest Shackleton took on his South Polar expedition. While Shackleton offered dutiful praise - "The car was extremely reliable and, notwithstanding the extreme temperatures of 30 degrees below zero, no breakages of any description occurred" - and bought a new Arrol-Johnston as soon as he returned to Britain, the ski car was only moderately successful.

After T C Pullinger took over as general manager the company moved south to a remarkable new factory at Heathhall, Dumfries. There was even a scheme to create a model village to house the workforce, but only 34 houses out of a planned 300 were ever built.

In 1920, Arrol-Johnston ventured into the light car market at Tongland, Kirkcudbrightshire. The most remarkable thing about the plant was that it was run by Pullinger's daughter Dorothée and almost entirely staffed by women, but that did not stop production ending there in 1922.

Indeed, the story of the Scottish car industry is one of almost continuous decline, of grand plans that failed to mature. Of more than sixty car makers that have operated in the country, the majority were active before the Great War; fourteen existed between the wars and post-1945 only seven or eight firms have built cars.

The most ambitious scheme of the postwar era was the Rootes plant at Linwood, Glasgow, the most northerly manifestation of the government policy of forcing car makers to site new factories in areas of high unemployment in the early 1960s. Linwood was the home of Project Ajax, the revolutionary rear-engined Hillman Imp, intended as a challenge to the recently-launched BMC Mini. But the plant proved uneconomic and was plagued by poor industrial relations, while the Imp was a flawed design which never achieved its potential. After Chrysler took over the Rootes Group in the 1960s, Linwood was gradually run down, finally closing in 1981 with the loss of 5,000 jobs.

And then there was the sad story of AC (Scotland), which tried to perpetuate the AC 3000ME after production of this mid-engined Ford V6-powered sports coupé had ended at Thames Ditton in 1984. Just seven cars were built and a plan to perpetuate the design as the Ecosse with Alfa Romeo power ended when the firm went out of business.

But in all this welter of unsifted history, the three 'A's of Scotland stand out in the same way as do the three 'P's of America - Packard, Peerless and Peirce-Arrow - for Argyll, Arrol-Johnston and Albion were the three makes which put Scotland on the international motoring map. They invariably listed their country of origin as Scotland, not Britain; Argylls talked of "export to England" in their press releases, and Arrol-Johnston in their racing days decked out their cars in tartan to compensate for the absence of Scottish national colours.

Like the best laid schemes of mice and men, it seems, the bold plans of Scotland's car makers have been fated to 'gang aft a-gley'...

Author's note

Jack Webster

In taking delivery of the first motor car imported to Scotland, in 1895, a minister's son from the Springburn district of Glasgow not only gave it his blessing but went on to produce his own version of this modern contraption, the first in Britain.

The same George Johnston gave his name to the Arrol-Johnston car - and was soon joined by other Scottish companies like Argyll, which became the biggest car manufacturer in Europe, and Albion, which survived longer than any.

Scotland's ability to produce great engineers was in evidence once more. But if the subsequent story failed to live up to the early promise, this small nation has still had a remarkable century of involvement with the motor car.

Apart from its manufacture, which reached a peak in the 1970s with mass production by Chrysler at Linwood, Scotland took to motor sport in a big way and gave the world some of its greatest names.

Jim Clark and Jackie Stewart became world-beating legends of the Grand Prix circuit, while the home-based Ecurie Ecosse sent drivers like Ron Flockhart and Ninian Sanderson to the gruelling test of Le Mans - and won on successive years.

In later generations, Colin McRae from Lanark triumphed as the first British man to win the world rallying championship - Louise Aitken-Walker from Duns had already won the women's rally title - and John Cleland, a garage-owner from Galashiels, was twice hailed as British touring car champion. Meanwhile, young talents like David Coulthard and Dario Franchitti had emerged as fresh aspirants to the crowns of Clark and Stewart.

These and many other stories have built into a history of spectacular achievement, colourful characters and rich romance which is told by word and picture in this book.

It sets out to tell this amazing story in a manner which will be understood by those who may know very little about motor cars but will appreciate the broad sweep of this great Scottish adventure. You are invited to settle yourself comfortably ...
IN THE DRIVING SEAT.

PREFACE

The publishers of this book have no intention of adding to the existing list of technical works on the history of the automobile. Such formal accounts of exclusive interest to the specialist reader have nothing in common with "In the Driving Seat".

Divested of all superfluous technicalities and clothed in a language of instant appeal to the everyday reader, it is difficult to find a subject so full of romance and thrills as the origin and development of roads, fuel and "everything on wheels".

This fascinating topic has been conceived between these covers from a special and unique point of view – a delving into the depths of history.

Designed for thinking people who delight in good literature, presented in a bright and absorbing form, it serves to show that history loses none of its interest to the specialist by being translated into a popular idiom.

The story is told in illustrations and anecdotes. It is a tale of intrigue, adventure, heroism and sacrifice with all the elements of the conventional "best seller" and the added advantage of being based on truth and experience. This "historical novel" gives the reader a peep behind the scenes of the Scottish car industry - one of the greatest theatres of action the world has ever experienced, and discloses secrets of startling interest even to those who think themselves "in the know."

Cover artist

Senga Murray was born in Hamilton and after graduating from Glasgow School of Art quickly became involved in the design and illustration of football club publicity material.

Her *Illustrated History of Glasgow Rangers Football Club* and other work adorn the corridors and rooms at Ibrox Stadium.

Other sporting fields saw Senga being commissioned to paint the great American golfer Arnold Palmer's portrait commemorating his 60th birthday. Senga is currently working towards a publication of *Scotland's Sporting Legends* by Bob Crampsey due to be launched in late 1997.

DESCRIPTION OF ARGYLL WORKS, ALEXANDRIA

Architecturally the outstanding feature of the Alexandria Works was and is the terracotta administration building facing the main road. When it was opened on June 26th 1906, its three gilded domes blinking in the sunlight, the building seemed more than a little grandiose compared with the size of the contemporary car-market. Three hundred guests were present at the opening of the works when Lord Montagu of Beaulieu performed the opening ceremony and was in the words of an account "astounded". To mark the opening Alexander Govan was presented with a rose-bowl in chased silver with a picture of the works beautifully engraved upon it as well as a clock and a pair of vases. It would be interesting to know if any of these items still survive.

Cover painting by Senga Murray

The Argyll – A Leader in Europe

The notion of a Scottish car industry performing, in the early days of motoring, as a tiddler on the edge of a world-class pool is very far off the mark. Indeed when the Argyll Motor company began producing its famous cars at Alexandria at the beginning of the century, it was turning out more vehicles than any other manufacturer in Europe.

Declaring the new car plant open in 1906, the widely experienced Lord Montagu of Beaulieu confirmed that it was the best-equipped in the world.

For certain, the Argyll company had raised by far the most impressive building, a piece of stunningly ornate architecture which could have been mistaken for a Czarist palace, the glorious facade of which remains in existence as we approach another century.

The Argyll company was not alone in setting the standards of a new and exciting industry. It merely typified the belief of a great engineering nation that, if it could do it for ships and locomotives, it could surely repeat the success with the new-fangled motor car.

It seemed a reasonable ambition and the early signs were set fair. As in so many of life's adventures, you soon latch on to the sheer enthusiasm, determination and foresight of one man when you seek out the origins of the Argyll cars.

Towards the end of a 19th century where road transport was still dominated by the horse-carriage and the bicycle, you find a young Scot called Alexander Govan going south to work for a cycle company at Redditch, near Birmingham. It was a time of exciting discovery when mankind was contemplating not only what could be achieved on land but was within a few years of defying gravity and taking to the air as well.

The cycle company in Redditch was turning its thoughts to the motor car, having brought in from the continent three models, a Vallee, a Benz and a Mors, which were studied in advance of bringing out a light vehicle of its own. The young Scot was already the works superintendent at the Redditch factory.

By 1899, however, Alexander Govan was back home where, by chance, a Glasgow entrepreneur, Warren Smith of the National Telegraph Company, found himself wondering what to do with the recently-defunct Scottish Cycle Company in Hozier Street, Bridgeton. Smith happened to know Govan and had no sooner consulted him than the two men were bursting into business, as chairman and managing director respectively, full of enthusiasm for the new industry which would revolutionise all human existence.

Even before that century was out, Govan had already

A 1900 model built at the Bridgeton factory
© Glasgow Museums

designed and built his first light car, the Argyll, the type of vehicle known in those days as a "voiturette," which could be bought for £250 and had a choice of three different engines and four body-styles.

With everyone watching everyone else, it seems that Govan had taken his closest look at the ideas of Louis Renault, while managing to escape any charge of infringement! He simply bought in other people's engines until he discovered how to build them himself. In 1902, for example, they ranged from 2hp to 6hp and came from De Dion and MMC but soon he was offering bigger sizes, having done a deal with the Aster company.

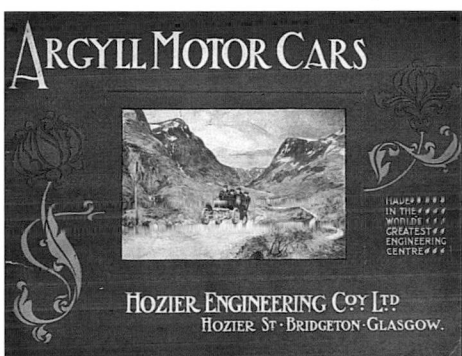

1904 catalogue cover
© Glasgow Museums

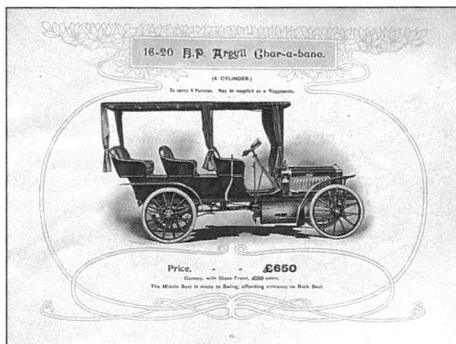

1904 model 16-20 hp Charabanc
© Glasgow Museums

The dynamic Govan had nothing to learn about the value of publicity and was to be found, prominently, at the wheel of his voiturette in the Scottish Automobile Club run of 1901. At the Glasgow International Exhibition of that same year the Argyll went through the five-day trials without losing a mark – and was soon knocking ten hours off the John-o'-Groats to Land's End record, establishing a time of 42 hours 5 minutes.

Production of

the Argyll was said to have reached 15 cars per week, with a range of choice which was wide and complicated (An American gent would yet show the beauty of simplifying your operations!)

But space at what was known as the Hozier Engineering Company was now at a premium and they had to look to the future. They struck on a 53-acre site at Alexandria and knew there would be plenty skilled labour in an area where the men had to travel more often to places like Dumbarton and Clydebank for work.

Good reserves had been built up and the venture was marked by high ambition when it went ahead in 1905, despite the caution that such moves have a habit of sowing the seeds of future destruction. It needed £250,000 to put up the main building and another £250,000 to meet production and start-up costs.

But the finished result was an impressive sight, striking from the outside and characterised by marble staircase and grand corridors on the inside. What's more, the over-all design had been conceived by the remarkable Govan himself, who had been to Europe and

1904 model 16-20 hp Tonneau
© Glasgow Museums

1904 model 10-12 hp Two Cylinder
© Glasgow Museums

Peter Burt, original inventor of the Single Sleeve Valve Engine as used in Argyll Cars
© George Oliver Archive

The Hozier Engineering Company have received the following cablegram from their Melbourne agents. "Australian 700 mile reliability trial, Argylls first and second".
Motor World - May 1905

Mr Andrew Carnegie has placed an order for a 24hp Argyll fitted with Rois de Belges side entrance body and canopy.
Motor World - May 1905

1897
The inaugural meeting of the Automobile Club of Great Britain was held on 5 December in Whitehall, London.

America and brought back ideas away ahead of their time, especially in terms of health and comfort for the workers.

Extensive heating and ventilation systems brought fresh warm air to all parts of the building. There were dining-rooms, recreation rooms, a reading room and hall for 500 people, wash-basins and lockers on a new-found scale.

Hot meals were served at reasonable prices and some measure of the social life at the Argyll works can be gauged from the fact that it soon had its own orchestra, a choir, ambulance class, cycling club, rifle club, a works magazine and such a large football interest that it had no fewer than 35 teams competing at five-a-side.

The Bridgeton coachbuilding shop
© Glasgow Museums

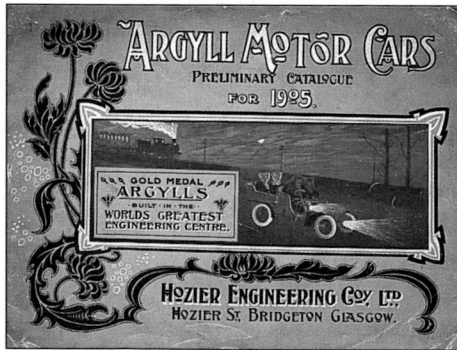

1905 catalogue cover
© Glasgow Museums

On the more immediate matter of production, the directors told their agents at a dinner in the famous Trocadero Restaurant in Glasgow that they were looking for an output of 1200 cars a year at the new factory. It was an ambitious target but in 1907 they were certainly turning out more than 800 cars a year, which was beyond anything being achieved by the other manufacturers in Europe. The work-force ranged from 1300 to 2000.

So the Scots were already significant players in the production of motor cars. Whether they were on the right lines is an easier matter for hindsight, keeping in mind the methods of mass production which would overtake the industry. The Alexandria works were undoubtedly built on such a scale but Alexander Govan's ways were more for the hand-built engine and the sheer craftsmanship for which Scottish engineering was already noted. The cars were well designed, immaculately turned out and strictly tested.

In the event, the Argyll Motor company was soon to run into an appalling tragedy. The new enterprise was no sooner on its way than its main driving force, the irrepressible Alexander Govan, collapsed and died at the age of 38. Some sources still put it down to a fatal attack of food poisoning, after a meal at the Grosvenor Restaurant in Glasgow, no doubt supported by the fact that his widow did sue the restaurant. But it later emerged that he had suffered a cerebral haemorrhage, with much speculation about the business burdens he was carrying, including the fact that Argyll was still well below its potential of output.

Whatever the situation, much of Alexandria's drive and purpose disappeared with Govan's death and within a year the

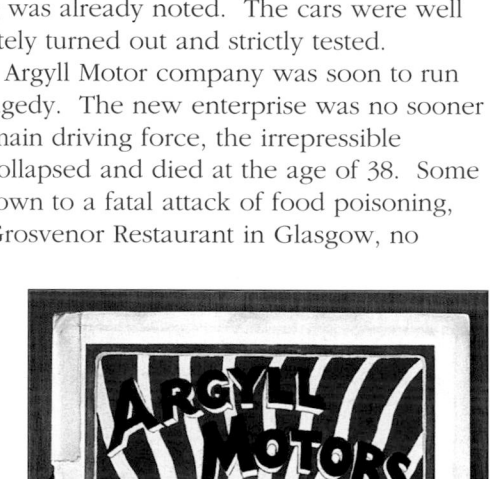

1906 Special Souvenir catalogue
© Glasgow Museums

Advertisement from the Motor-Car World, March 1903

The Hozier Engineering Company is the first Scottish firm to show in Paris. The principal exhibit a tonneau driven by a 3 cylinder 12 hp motor of their own make. The stand was in a good position in the great nave and the handsome Argyll stood comparison with any car within the vicinity.
Motor World - January 1904

1898
The Madelvic electric brougham is built.

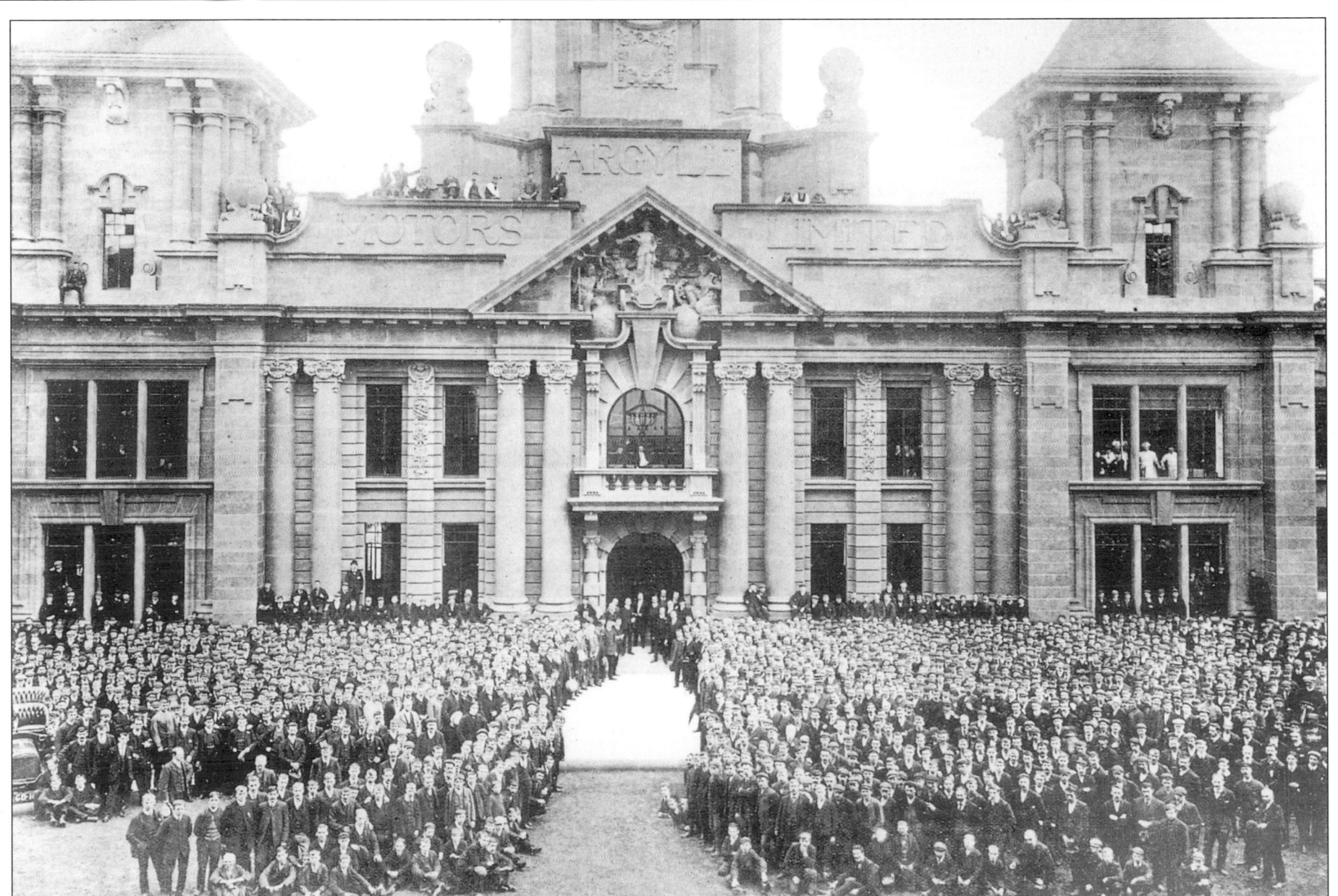

The Inauguration of the new Argyll Works at Alexandria

© National Motor Museum, Beaulieu

company went into voluntary liquidation, with a deficit of £360,000.

A new package was devised, however, and the work continued with a new managing director, Colonel John Matthew, who was put there by the Dunlop Rubber Company, principal creditor of the old company.

A gentleman called Henri Perrot became chief designer and work proceeded apace, even though a large part of the work-force had now been paid off. There was a success with a new 12hp model – they even exported 50 cabs to New York – but Argyll was still producing too many models.

In 1909 Colonel Matthew took an interest in developing the single sleeve-valve invented by a Glasgow engineer, Peter Burt, which was generally accepted as having been ahead of its time. By unfortunate coincidence, a Canadian engineer had patented a similar design just ahead of Burt but the two men reached agreement and came up with the Burt-McCollum single sleeve-valve engine.

It took Henri Perrot two years to develop the new engine but it became an undoubted success, as witness what happened in 1913 when the Argyll car set out for the famous Brooklands Track to establish long-distance records which did not then exist.

The famous Benz driver called Horsted, and another called Scott, alternated at the wheel of this racing Argyll and, on two days at the end of May 1913, they set up some very impressive Class D records.

On the first occasion, they drove more than 1000 miles in 14 hours at an average speed of 72.59 mph. A week later, despite a thunderstorm which flooded the track, the "hour" was raised to 78.29 mph. The Argyll's fastest lap was was actually 82.45 mph – not bad going in 1913!

By this time, however, a drawn-out courtroom battle with Daimler over patents brought £50,000 worth of costs – Argyll had won their case and the company could ill afford a legal bill like that.

Unfortunately, a venture into aero engines, which again seemed to be the way to progress, proved to be the last straw. Financial troubles mounted and in 1914 the company went into liquidation, passing to the Admiralty for £153,000 and becoming a munitions factory for the First World War.

Angry creditors condemned the management and said

Detail of the fine sculpture above the main entrance at Alexandria

© George Oliver archive

they were "not fit to run a hen-coop!" This was virtually the end of the great Argyll enterprise though John Brimlow, the company's sales manager in Glasgow, did take over the old Bridgeton works and continue to give the car a form of life until 1928. But it was all a pale shadow of its former self.

The Navy returned in 1935 and the Alexandria works became a torpedo factory until 1969 (by coincidence, one of the Argyll models was known as the Torpedo).

As for the magnificent building, there were various high hopes and false starts in the years that followed but the great edifice fell into disrepair, though standing defiant in the face of the vandals. Trees and weeds continued to sprout from the old masonry.

As Dumbarton District Council sought a solution for its famous listed building the brightest prospect arose in 1996 when Classical House, the company which developed the Glasgow Italian Centre, acquired the edifice and asked permission to develop it. The idea was for a complex of quality retailing outlets, 20 lettable spaces for well-known designer labels and so on.

In the midst of all that contemporary jargon, the company did have the sensitivity to respect the brief but extraordinary history of the Argyll building.

Retaining the facade, they were also planning a visitors' centre to show succeeding generations that there was once a major motor car industry behind these walls. It had been a glorious episode while it lasted but, as too often in the Scottish experience, it came unstuck in the end.

There is one fascinating footnote to the story of the Argyll car factory. Among the apprentices at Alexandria were two young lads who would soon make their own mark in the wider world. One was Harry Ferguson, who would develop the famous tractor - and the other was John Logie Baird from Helensburgh, the inventor of television.

1907 catalogue cover showing the Alexandria Works
© Glasgow Museums

1907 four cylinder Limousine
© Glasgow Museums

1900
Designer Herbert Austin presented the first four-wheeled Wolseley in January.

1907 model 12-14 hp (four cylinder) Argyll
© Glasgow Museums

1912 model 12 hp Doctor's coupé
© Glasgow Museums

1914 model Streamline Limousine
© Glasgow Museums

1914 model 15/30 hp Streamline Landauette
© Glasgow Museums

1914 model 15 hp 4-cylinder Cab
© Glasgow Museums

Entrance Hall, Argyll Works, Alexandria
© Glasgow Museums

1908 Light Argyll Van with the houses of Govan Drive, Alexandria named after the founder
© Glasgow Museums

Argyll Fire Engine outside the Alexandria Factory in 1908
© Glasgow Museums

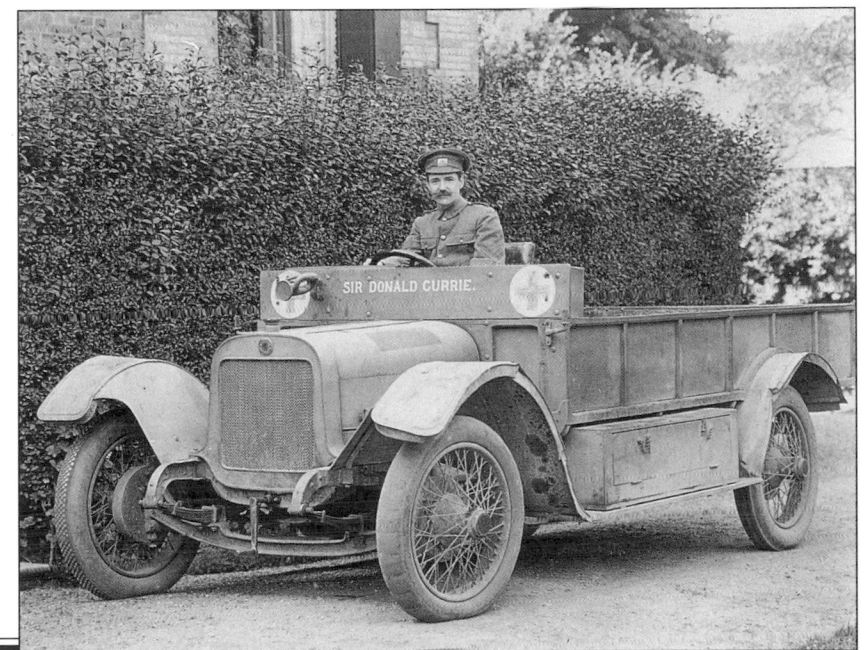

World War One Argyll Ambulance
© Glasgow Museums

Motor Mary of Argyll.

(Lines addressed to a car of that ilk after a journey from Glasgow to London.)

I have risen up to greet thee
Very early in the morn
At the Central Hotel, Glasgow,
In thy cushioned body borne.
To thy home among the Highlands,
To thy new ancestral halls,
Where the staircase can out-marble
Even Pall Mall club house walls.
I have taken petrol with thee
At thy afternoon "at home",
And have gazed upon thy workshops
And thy silent golden dome.

I have Journeyed with thee, Mary,
By the banks and braes and burns
Of Loch Lomond, and have taken
all the gradients and turns.
Through the passes of the mountains,
With a glow, of speedy joy,
In the scenes where fights and slaughters
Were the pastime of Rob Roy.
I have "rested and been thankful"
Just beyond the hairpin bend,
With "The Old Bear" as a mascot,
Guide, philosopher and friend.

I have travelled back to London
In a run of twenty hours
With thyself, "sweet fifteen" Mary,
And thy magic petrol powers.
And thou never, Highland Mary,
Seemed to suffer from the cold,
Though my own poor "little Mary"
Could another tale have told.
Rough and smooth you took the journey
With an everlasting smile
From the silence of your gear-teeth,
Motor Mary of Argyll.

Fred Gillett

1913 model 15/30 hp Type 'G'
© Glasgow Museums

1927 model in the grounds of Pollok House
© Glasgow Museums

The 15hp Argyll car might fittingly be termed the complete touring car. Its equipment includes a luncheon and tea outfit, valance boxes for carrying tools and spare parts and mackintosh coats, and a special case for carrying ladies hats fitted behind the driver's seat. The car is fitted with the new Dynamo lighting set.
Motor World - December 1910

Visitors to the Knickerbocker Hotel, the Carlton of New York, will be struck by the smart appearance and comfort of the Argyll taxi-cabs which are always in readiness at the doors of this luxurious hotel. Although 50 of these cabs have been on the New York streets for up to four years, they are as good as ever and universally recognised as the best taxi-cabs in the city.
Motor World - September 1911

1901
The Cadillac Car Company was formed in Detroit, USA, while in Britain the first diesel engine went on display.

The Argyll Octogenarian

It is doubtful if Alex Govan, John Brimlow, Peter Burt or John Matthew, these stalwarts of Argyll Motors Limited, could ever have thought of a more appropriate home for the last remaining Argyll still running in Scotland.

This 1910, 10 hp, 2 cylinder model, still in magnificent condition, is owned by Onich-born Donald Cameron who lives in the lovely Argyll village of St Catherines looking over Loch Fyne to Inveraray Castle, home of the Duke of Argyll.

The car was bought by Donald in 1985 from Roy Middleton in England, whose uncle, incidentally, had been the last manager of the Argyll Motor Company of London. A metal plate shows that the car was originally supplied by the Parkstone Motor Company of Poole, Dorset, a firm which to this day is still in business.

LU5684, this gracious sedate lady, with her shining blue bonnet carries her years on the roads with great pride and it is no surprise to hear Donald Cameron and his wife Sandra say that they wouldn't swap it for the dearest Rolls-Royce.

Donald & Sandra Cameron in their Argyll
Courtesy of Donald Cameron

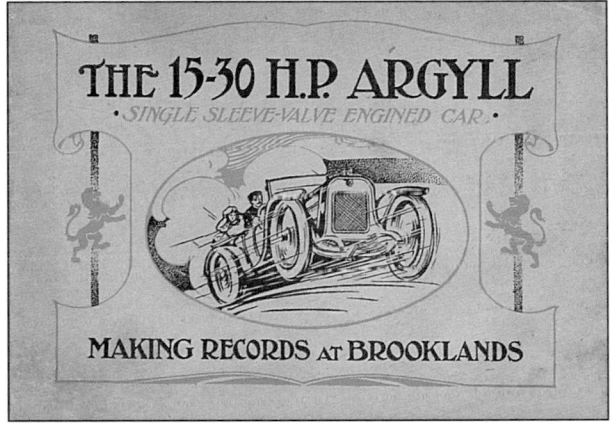

Cover of an Argyll brochure produced to mark the record breaker at Brooklands in 1913
© Glasgow Museums

1908 Argyll Tourer driven by Frank Thomson, winner of the Concours d'Elegance Dewar Trophy in the 1993 Veteran Car Club's Scottish Rally seen here at Inveraray Castle with the Duke of Argyll
Courtesy of Donald Cameron

One of the most interesting features of the traffic in Princes Street in Edinburgh is the service of motor cars between the Post Office and the Haymarket. Standing near Scott's Monument the other day the writer saw six cars pass in about as many minutes all full up with passengers. The Laird of Barnbogle, by which Lord Roseberry is known in a certain district, has been motoring a good deal about Edinburgh recently. With two ex-Premiers and the Prime Minister on its side the automobile may be expected to survive the antagonism of Sir Henry Campbell-Bannerman as expressed by him in Stirlingshire on one occasion.
Motor World - August 1902

Mr Harry Lauder, the well-known Scottish comedian, is now the owner of a 12/16hp Decauville car.
Motor World - 13 May 1905

1902
The new, pace-setting 35 hp Mercedes, with powerful front-mounted engine catapulted the Mercedes design ahead of Panhard.

Arrol-Johnston – The Mo-Car Men

If the Argyll can claim to be the best-remembered car from that early part of the century, it was just one of the three big 'A's which dominated the pioneering days of Scotland's flirtation with this new and exciting industry. The others were the Arrol-Johnston and the Albion, though the latter company quickly moved from cars to commercial vehicles.

The very first car imported to Scotland, in 1895, was owned by a minister's son from the Springburn district of Glasgow, George Johnston, appropriate since his name would take its place in motor car history as one half of that Arrol-Johnston company which became the first major manufacturer of cars in the land.

The other half of the name belonged to Sir William Arrol, the distinguished Glasgow engineer whose name had recently gained fame around the world as builder of the spectacular Forth Bridge, having previously built the replacement for the Tay Bridge at Dundee, following the rail disaster of 1879.

Aficionados of the motor car, who are legion, will tell you that, strictly speaking, George Johnston was not the first manufacturer of cars in Scotland. They will point to people like John Stirling of Hamilton, who had produced his first motor carriage in 1896. Stirling, however, was not an engineer, didn't even gain much mechanical knowledge but bought in Daimler chassis for his family coachbuilding company to attach a body of the customer's choosing.

There were also romantic stories, like that of Postie Lawson of Craigievar in Aberdeenshire, the local postmaster, who built his "Craigievar Express" in 1897. As recently as 1971 it covered the distance from London to Brighton and became an exhibit at the Grampian Transport Museum at Alford, Aberdeenshire.

None of that, however, detracts from the significance of George Johnston, whose father came of farming stock in Berwickshire while his mother was a daughter of Hugh Fulton, an enterprising farmer-cum-businessman from Eaglesham.

George was just a small boy when his father became United Presbyterian minister at Springburn, with a substantial manse called Mosesfield House on Balgray Hill.

Without any background of engineering in the family, young George trained at the Hydepark Locomotive Company

The A-J radiator badge
© Glasgow Museums

1903
The birth of Vauxhall and Ford. Vauxhall Iron Works announced its first car, a 5 hp voiturette priced at 130 guineas. Over the Atlantic, Henry started the Ford Motor Company.

The famous Arrol-Johnston 1901 Dog Cart
© Glasgow Museums

in Springburn but spread his interest to creating machinery for Brown and Polson of Paisley, the cornflour and custard powder people, as well as machinery for making pandrops.

In 1894, when Glasgow Corporation was seeking to bring in a steam tramcar in place of the horse-drawn one, George Johnston was well enough known to be given the assignment. In the test-run, however, the tram went on fire and the idea was abandoned.

By now his enthusiasm was all for the motor car and by 1895 he was stripping down a Panhard-Levassor in the coach-house of the Springburn manse. Examining what other people were doing, Johnston concluded he could do better himself and by 1896 was well on his way with design and construction.

To form what was at first known as the Mo-Car Company, he enlisted the financial backing of Sir William Arrol and several members of the Coats family of Paisley (Arrol's father had started as a cotton-spinner but rose to be manager of one of the Coats mills).

So Johnston became the instigator of the first British-built motor car, to be joined in the company by his cousin, Norman Osborne Fulton, who was in charge of assembly and manufacture, and his friend T Blackwood Murray, an electrical engineer who had been works manager with Mavor and Coulson.

In fact Murray was experimenting with an all-electric car but it was the petrol model which took the eye, tackling the one-in-five climb on Douglas Street, Glasgow, and reaching speeds of 17mph on the flat.

But Fulton and Murray were finding it difficult to get on with Johnston and began planning a different future for themselves. Fulton went first to America to gain further experience but returned in time to team up with Murray as they embarked on the creation of that third name in Scottish motor manufacturing - the Albion Motor Car Company.

Meanwhile, the Arrol-Johnston venture, registered in 1899 with a capital of £50,000, was producing cars at its works in the Camlachie district of the city and focussing on a 12hp six-

A very early use of motor vehicles instead of horses and carts. This 1904 photograph shows an Arrol-Johnston lorry and a Wolseley van both of the Castlebank Laundry.
© Nigel Kennedy

1905 Arrol-Johnston TT Model '18' 4 litre The prototype driven by General Manager J S Napier won the first Isle of Man Tourist Trophy race in September 1905 at an average speed of 33.9 mph.
© Glasgow Museums

1908 Arrol-Johnston 12 hp air-cooled, specially built for Sir Ernest Shackleton's South Pole expedition.
© National Motor Museum, Beaulieu

The famous 1909 model 15.9 hp Arrol-Johnston
© Glasgow Museums

seater dogcart with a heavy chassis.

But the Camlachie building was destroyed by fire in 1901, removing all drawings and records, and car production moved to the disused Underwood threadmill in Paisley, provided by the Coats family. Despite the loss of drawings and patterns, work resumed quite successfully, though Johnston himself seemed to be less involved.

By then that remarkable Scot, William Beardmore, who was once responsible for more than 40,000 jobs on Clydeside, had gained control of the company, with J S Napier as managing director. They were seeking to improve the old-fashioned look of the car.

This new-found industry was often a matter of short durations and it is surprising to find that this man who instigated the first British car, George Johnston, had left his company altogether as early as 1904.

Two events of 1909 helped boost the fortunes of the Arrol-Johnston company. First, Sir Ernest Shackleton returned from his famous South Pole Expedition with reports of high success from the special vehicles which Arrol-Johnston produced for the hazardous journey.

Then the company found a man of destiny with the arrival of Thomas Pullinger as general manager. Pullinger was another of those energetic young men whose astonishing ingenuity carves them out distinguished careers.

Having worked at the Woolwich Arsenal, he set out for France in search of work and became a designer with Alexander Darracq, who would become a famous name in that early motor industry, turning out tourers like the 8hp model which starred in the film of "Genevieve."

Pullinger returned to Britain as manager of the Sunbeam Motor Company and moved on to Humber before taking over as works manager and designer for Arrol-Johnston at Paisley. He was then 43. Within a year he was managing director, planning to move production from Paisley to Dumfries, with the explanation that it would be nearer the English market while retaining the Scottish identity.

Pullinger bought a deer forest at Heathhall, Dumfries, and

having taken a look at Henry Ford's buildings in the United States, engaged an American company to put up Britain's first-ever ferro-concrete factory.

It was producing cars by 1913 but, with the outbreak of the First World War a year later, Arrol-Johnston and other manufacturers were switched to shells and aero-engines, which Pullinger helped to develop. All this gave work to 1500 people in Dumfries, with a weekly wage bill of £9000.

By the time the war ended they were ready with a new model, the Victory costing £700, one of the early cars being delivered to the Prince of Wales. But the Victory was a flop and the Prince's car was returned to the company. The model was scrapped.

Pullinger concentrated on a light car called the Galloway, built first at Tongland, Kirkcudbright, and later at Heathhall. He had also given the company success with a 15.9hp Arrol-Johnston. But in the post-war world the drift was towards mass production and life became increasingly difficult. That 15.9 Arrol-Johnston which cost £625 in 1920 was down to £385 by 1928. Compared to that, the Morris Oxford tourer, with its much higher output, was costing £315 – and the Model T Ford was selling as a tourer for £150.

Thomas Pullinger retired in 1926 and a year later Arrol-Johnston merged with the Aster Engineering Company of Wembley. But trouble was looming. The market for custom-built cars had declined and the re-organised Arrol-Aster went into liquidation in 1929, ceasing to exist in 1931. The Dumfries factory later came into the ownership of the Uniroyal company.

William Beardmore, who became Lord Invernairn, ran his own separate company as well as the Arrol-Johnston involvement, producing taxi-cabs, light vans and engines for commercial vehicles. In 1919 he began turning out his taxis from the former Arrol-Johnston factory in Paisley. It was a successful venture which set the pattern of taxis for years to come. By 1928 more than 6000 had been supplied to London alone.

As a footnote to the Arrol-Johnston story, the founding George Johnston was not only the first man in Scotland to own a car, he was also the first to be charged with a city motoring offence.

He was driving his horseless carriage through the centre of Glasgow, at the junction of Argyle Street and St Enoch's Square at a time when such vehicles were not permitted. The man who gave Scotland its first car was fined half-a-crown!

Main entrance to the new Arrol-Johnston factory at Heathhall, Dumfries
© Glasgow Museums

Cover of the 1914 catalogue
© Glasgow Museums

1906
The French Auto Club's first Grand Prix was staged on the Circuit de la Sarthe at Le Mans, with Sisz averaging 63 mph on a Renault to win.

1920 Arrol-Johnston 15.9hp car - one of the few remaining Dumfries built models.
© Glasgow Museums

1922 Arrol-Johnston 15.9 hp allweather tourer at the entrance to the former Heathhall factory. Body built by Penman of Dumfries.
© George Oliver archive

I AM, THOU ART, HE IS, WE ARE, YOU ARE, THEY ARE

Going to Olympia to see the New

ARROL·JOHNSTON CARS.

The Type of Car which gained First and Fourth Places in the Tourist Trophy Race is on view at Stands 35 and 40.

24 H.P. NEW ARROL-JOHNSTON TONNEAU.

PLEASE SEND FOR CATALOGUE No. 14.

THE . . .
NEW ARROL-JOHNSTON CAR Co., Ltd.,
PAISLEY, SCOTLAND.

Advert from 'The Motor' magazine November 1905
© Glasgow Museums

1907
Ford's Model T, although not yet in production in the UK, made its debut at the Olympia show in October, on importer Percy Perry's stand.

1925 and 1926 Arrol-Johnston catalogue covers and contents

© Glasgow Museums

When stopped by a policeman while motoring in Hampshire towards the end of last month, Sir Thomas Lipton expressed a hope that he would not be summoned as he had to go to Scotland to attend to the Shamrock "so I see in the newspapers" said the constable "and I assure you Sir Thomas that if your yacht goes as fast in the race as your motor car did you are bound to win". Though the court laughed heartily at the recital, Sir Thomas's driver was fined £5 and costs of the same amount. This conviction was the second obtained against the driver at the same court by the same policeman!
Motor World - April 1903

1908
Home grown innovator Lanchester introduced a steering wheel on its larger car but preferred tiller steering for the smaller car.

Albion – Sure as the Sunrise

When you come to the third of the big 'A's in the history of the Scottish motor industry, you are dealing with the one which proved most consistent of all - the only one to survive the two world wars: the Albion Motor Company.

Albion became a major name in lorries and buses and, blessed with sound management, could once claim to be the biggest maker of motor vans in the British Empire.

It had all come from that decision of Norman Fulton and Thomas Blackwood Murray to leave the pioneering George Johnston and break out on their own. They did so with only two days to spare before the arrival of the year 1900, establishing the company which would take on the name of Albion, once used to describe the British Isles.

While Fulton was a cousin of George Johnston, he was also the brother-in-law of his new partner in business, T Blackwood Murray. And it was Murray's father who took out a bond on his farm at Heavyside, near Biggar, which would guarantee the young men in their venture.

The original Albion premises occupied the first floor and attic of the Clan Line repair shop at the foot of Finnieston Street in Glasgow, where they employed seven men. Murray designed the car throughout, with the initial object of creating a petrol engine. Among his designs, he produced a most reliable type of low-tension magneto.

Those early employees worked away at that first Albion model which appeared with an 8hp engine in 1900. By 1902 they were producing 35 chassis and selling their cars as far away as Kuala Lumpur. For that very first chassis, even Murray's farming father had weighed in by machining some parts on his lathe at Biggar.

You can imagine the excitement as completion date approached, with much late night work to see the first car on the road. It was evidently at 3 o'clock one morning when it was finally ready. Fulton and Murray didn't wait. From those upstairs premises they took it down on the hoist, cranked it up and were off along Stobcross Street in a bustle of enthusiasm.

Alas, there was a loud noise and the car came to a halt. A fractured bracket attached to the rear axle had caused the problem and the two entrepreneurs withdrew to an all-night dockland coffee-house to gather their thoughts. Within a few days, however, they had put right the fault and set out on the 40-mile journey to Biggar, forced to stop every 12 miles or so to fill up with water.

The new car was soon proving its reliability, picking up a major Automobile Club award during the Glasgow International Exhibition of 1901. As they broke into the export market, the A2 model of 1902 became available as a car and an 8hp half-ton van. By another year they were moving to a factory at Scotstoun and, from then on, the Albion story was one of progress through dependability, incorporating a motif and a motto which said "Sure as the Sunrise."

Production built up, with more and more heavy goods vehicles, till the company was employing 283 people in 1906 and 450 a few years later. An Albion motor, they were telling the world, would survive for well upwards of 150,000 miles or ten years.

By now you would find this sturdy Scots model in any

Albion radiator badge
© Albion Archive, Biggar

1908 Albion Pleasure Car
© Albion Archive, Biggar

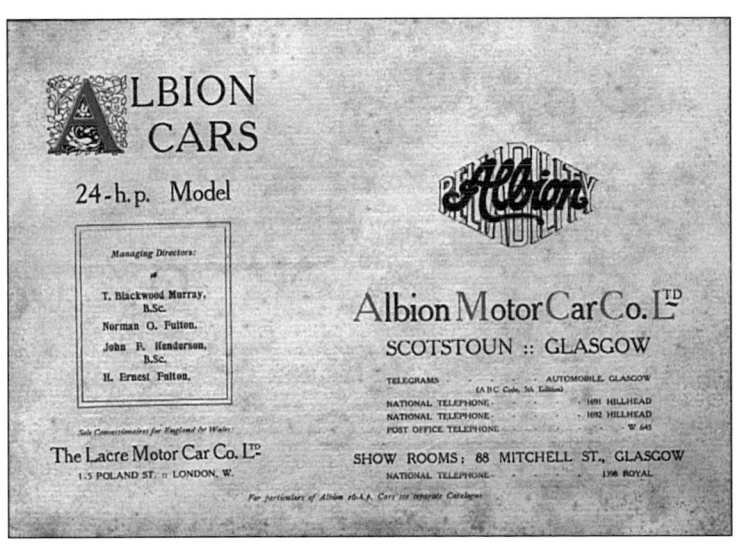

Frontispiece from the 1908 catalogue
© Glasgow Museums

part of the empire. In London, a company called the Long Acre Motor Car Company (Lacre) helped to establish the Albion name and you would find the famous Harrods store lining up an impressive array of 100 vans from the Glasgow factory. But soon the Lacre company was a competitor, making complete vehicles of its own.

In 1910 Albion introduced the 3/4-ton A10 model of 32hp, which became the staple product. By 1913 there was a 25-seater charabanc (the early name for a bus).

Of the 554 Albions made in 1912, about 150 were cars. The trend was becoming clear and before the outbreak of the First World War the directors had decided that they would concentrate on producing heavy goods vehicles. It was another sign of shrewd business acumen, taking notice of what was happening to companies like Argyll.

During the Great War they turned out more than 6000 of the A10 lorries for the war effort.

An able man, T Blackwood Murray, who had gained a civil engineering degree at Edinburgh in 1890, was given an

honorary Doctor of Science by his old university in 1917.

By now all the major companies seemed to be running Albions. Along the side of their vehicles you would find every name from Lyon's Tea, Fry's Chocolate and McVitie and Price to Huntley and Palmer, BP, Nestlé and White Horse Whisky. While many another company foundered, Albion battled against the traumas of the post-war world and survived.

T Blackwood Murray eventually went to live in Switzerland where he died in 1929 after a long illness. His partner, Norman Fulton, survived until 1935, when he left an estate worth £141,000.

In the Depression of 1931, a bold advertisement compared Albion's Viking bus with the ocean liner Empress of Britain. They were both "Clyde-built – supreme examples of the finest engineering in the world."

In that same year, Albion produced a new family of chassis, with more of the letter V to follow the fashion. the

Lord Carmichael, Governor of Victoria, Australia, and his wife and daughter, with their 1908 Albion 24 hp at State House.
© Albion Archive, Biggar

An early Albion commercial vehicle poster
© Albion Archive, Biggar

1910
C S Rolls, the co-founder of Rolls-Royce was killed tragically in an air crash at the Bournemouth Aviation Meeting.

1911 Albion 16 hp van as used by Harrods of London
© Albion Archive, Biggar

Valkyrie, the Valiant and the Victor. Another of the V-letter, the Venturer, could once claim to be the only type of double-decker bus running in Australia.

In the early-to-mid thirties Albion was employing 1650 people in Glasgow and 300 more at depots around the country – and picking up a Royal Warrant for supplying lorries to King George V at Balmoral. It also expanded to another factory at Yoker in 1935.

The Halley vehicle had been a threat to Albion and there was a time, before the First World War, when that company was actually turning out more vehicles. But its position weakened and the field was left to Albion in 1926 when Halley went into liquidation. One of the latter's model names, the Chieftain, was taken up for an improved 5/6-ton Albion lorry in 1949. Albion had again been prominent in producing vehicles for the Second World War but faced a vastly changing world after the peace of 1945.

The early 1950s was a time of motor mergers. Austin and Morris came together in 1951 and Leyland began a major expansion which resulted in the take-over of the Albion Motor Company. In the mid-fifties Albion was turning out thousands of vehicles per year at Scotstoun and Yoker after Leyland had spent millions on new equipment. Progress

continued through the 1960s when the workforce reached 3500 and buses were being exported all over the world. Albion was also producing more and more components for the entire Leyland group.

In 1972, however, major changes brought Albion the new name of Leyland (Glasgow) and by 1980 the company was assembling vehicles no more. The Yoker factory was closed but, while no more vehicles would bear the name of Albion, the axle facilities of the whole group were concentrated on Glasgow and there was still work for 1100 people.

The troubles which would develop by another decade could perhaps be traced to 1987, when the state-owned Leyland trucks was privatised. The company badly needed a strong parent but a deal was done to make the UK Leyland business a subsidiary of the Dutch company DAF, which was never going to fill that role.

In 1993 the Leyland-DAF enterprise collapsed and the future of the Albion works at Scotstoun hung in the balance. Out of the turmoil, however, came an imaginative deal, put together by the Receivers, Arthur Andersen, in which a management team, led by chief executive Dan

Female employee at the Scotstoun works during WWI
© Albion Archives, Biggar

1910 Albion butcher's van
© Glasgow Museums

LMS Albion lorry (late 1920s) loading bales of wool.
© Albion Archive, Biggar

Dan Wright MBE
BSc CEng FIMechE
Born in Glasgow in 1949, Dan Wright began his career as a Graduate Trainee with the Ford Motor Company in 1971. After a number of posts he led the team which established Albion Automotive as an independent business in November 1993. Married with two children his recreational interests are shooting, hill-walking and driving cars and heavy trucks!

Wright, set out to rescue the Glasgow operation.

The good old name was revived as Albion Automotive and the creditors of the old company were persuaded to take equity holdings in the new venture. Dan Wright, a Scot who had previously been managing director and co-founder of Fleming Thermodynamics, brought a new spirit to Albion and led his team with a confidence which enabled them to acquire Farington Components of Lancashire, suppliers of parts for Volvo buses.

Booming sales brought new jobs in the mid-1990s, with work based on those famous axles and an investment programme to give promise for the future.

In a Scotland which had such high hopes of its motor industry at the turn of the century, it was left to the name of Albion to stay the course and seek to complete that century. As a sign of the quality which distinguished the product, you will still find the old Albion giving reliable service in distant parts of the world today.

Albion Model 24 car. Restored in 1958 by original bodybuilders, Penman of Dumfries.
© Albion Archive, Biggar

1912
The 956 mile race run over 10 laps of the Dieppe-Londinieres-En Triangle route in July was won by Boillot's Peugeot. Sunbeams however came 3rd, 4th and 5th.

With the locality so closely connected to the origins of the Albion Motor Company, Biggar Museum Trust naturally focussed its tribute to the pioneers on the centenary of the company in 1999.

For that purpose the Trust, which has more museums per head of population than anywhere in Scotland, including Glasgow, began to build up its collection of Albion vehicles many years in advance. That was achieved from the proceeds of the successful Vintage and Veteran Rally held every August, when around 300 vehicles head for Biggar.

Those taking part in the run travel over some of the first roads in Scotland to feel the impact of a petrol-driven vehicle. For it was on those same routes that many of the Mo-Car and Albion prototypes travelled in the early days to Biggar, where Albion's T Blackwood Murray and his family originated.

The earliest Albion in the Trust's collection is a 1902 dog cart car with tiller steering, similar to the one which Murray's father, a Biggar architect and farmer, drove a round trip of 1500 miles from Biggar to London, via the coast, in 1903. Then there is a fine wee hotel bus of 1923, used in the first Doctor Finlay television series, and a mobile home of 1938, built on the prototype chassis of the famous CX range.

Those centenary plans for the Albion Motor Company in 1999 were well worked out in advance: A run from London up the Great North Road to the Commercial Vehicle Museum at Leyland, then over the old Shap road into Scotland and on to Biggar, with the final lap ending at the works in Scotstoun.

Biggar can claim to have the surviving archives of the company, together with photographs and other records, which are all available for inspection by appointment.

The Albion Club is at Biggar as well, catering for the hundreds of enthusiasts in Britain and as far away as Australia, where Albions have survived in great numbers. Yes, there is even one in Alice Springs.

Advertisement in Motor-Car World, February 1903

1900 Albion 8 hp Model A2 Dog Cart with N O Fulton at the controls and T Blackwood-Murray as passenger

© Glasgow Museums

1913

The Morris Oxford was a Manchester Motor Show star. Most of its components were bought in and it had a longer wheelbase than in the initial design to fit a dickey seat: "The excellence impresses one immediately", the motoring press commented.

Albion – Sure as the Sunrise

A typical Albion lorry of the late 1920s.
Seen restored at a rally at Glamis Castle.
© George Oliver Archive

1923 Albion Model 20 "Pride of Tannochbrae" at the Albion Heritage Centre, Biggar. This was the Aberfeldy hotel bus and starred in the first "Dr Finlay's Casebook" TV series.
© Albion Archive, Biggar

Albion 'Viking' 24 hp 19 seater Motor Charabanc seen at Crianlarich Hotel in 1924.
© Glasgow Museums

Albion light vans delivering the Princess Royal's wedding cake in 1924
© Albion Archive, Biggar

Albion bus delivered to an Egyptian school about 1924.
© Albion Archive, Biggar

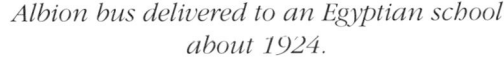
Albions deliver the Princess Royal's Wedding Cake, 1924.

1914
"This", wrote Charles Harper, 'Autocar's' war zone reporter, "is an automobile war" – referring to the massive mobilisation of cars for Britain's military campaign.

Albion – Sure as the Sunrise

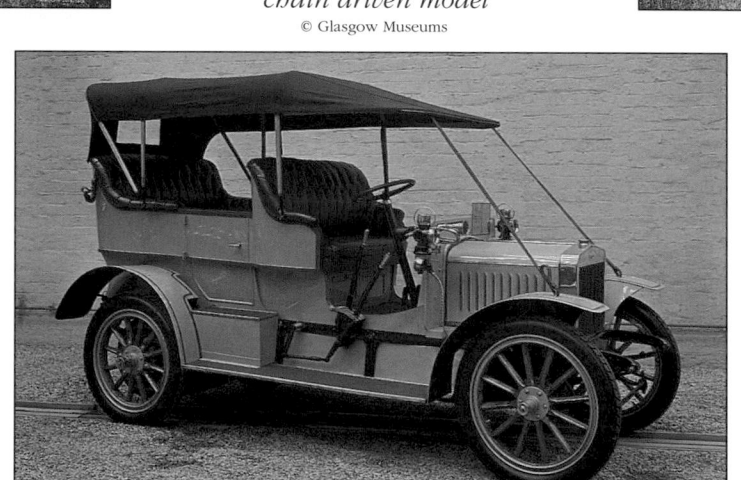

MAIL CAR LEAVING POST OFFICE, SCOURIE.

1904 Albion Mail Car leaving Scourie Post Office
in the North of Scotland
© National Motor Museum, Beaulieu

*Albion A3 1910 16hp Tourer - a double
chain driven model*
© Glasgow Museums

*1908 Albion 24-30 hp seen in the 1908 Scottish
Reliability Trial at Loch Lomond.*
© National Motor Museum, Beaulieu

Albion army vehicle of the late 1930s.
© Albion Archive, Biggar

*1933 Albion van and 1936 Albion lorry in use at
Castlebank Laundry, Anniesland. The streamlined
lorry was designed by Holland Coachcraft and used
the laundry's Fleur de Lys logo as the radiator grille
design.*
© Nigel Kennedy

WWI

*Motor car owners readily embraced the
war effort: R G Merry, chauffeured
General Gouvand and later became a
lieutenant, Oscar Thompson rebodied his
1907 Austin Brooklands Racer as an
ambulance. Arrol-Johnston, anxious that
its workers shouldn't be seen as shirkers
provided uniforms to wear while they
constructed aero engines. Crossley built
staff cars for the War Office, as did
Vauxhall which even opened a repair shop
in Petrograd, Russia.*

Albion 24hp 30 cwt Subsidy type van
© Glasgow Museums

Rear axle assembly at the new Albion Automotive plant in Scotstoun and although only established in 1993, the Glasgow operation has almost 100 years of history which began with Albion Motors Ltd in the production of high quality commercial vehicles.

© Albion Automotive, Scotstoun

Albion 32hp Mk II 3 ton lorry
© Glasgow Museums

Albion HL126 lorry of 1936 vintage seen here on the 1991 London - Brighton Commercial Run
© Albion Archive, Biggar

Albion FT37L Chieftain lorry built in 1951. It formed part of the Albion Guard of Honour which welcomed The Princess Royal when she opened Moat Park Heritage Centre, Biggar in 1988.
© Albion Archive, Biggar

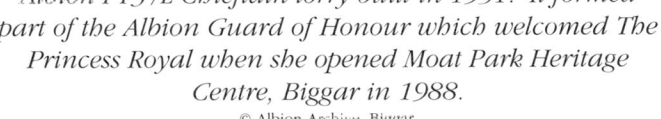

1919
Alcock & Brown were first to fly across the Atlantic Ocean in a Vickers Vimy powered by a Rolls-Royce engine shortly followed by the R34 airship.

Motor Car Fever

The three big 'A's of motor manufacture in Scotland – Argyll, Arrol Johnston and Albion - may have caught the headlines but around the turn of the century there was not a district in the land without somebody who was trying to produce his own version of this new contraption.

Motor car fever was everywhere and even before 1900 there were several models designed and produced with names which would linger for a time at least. But much of the enthusiasm ended after a few years, sometimes with only a handful of vehicles actually produced.

The **Madelvic** Motor Company was founded in 1898 by William Peck, who was Astronomer Royal for Scotland, based in Edinburgh. He built his premises along the road at Granton and believed that electricity would provide the best means of power for a road vehicle.

1898 Madelvic
© Glasgow Museums

So he produced what was not strictly a car, more an electric brougham driven by a central fifth wheel. He used it to run a public transport service between Granton and Leith and also turned out a vehicle for the Post Office. The Madelvic carriage was provided with shafts for a horse!

However the company was short-lived, deep in financial trouble as early as 1900.

John **Stirling** from Hamilton was one of the early pioneers of the motor industry in Scotland. He never made a complete vehicle but brought in popular engines and chassis and gave us, for example, the Stirling-Daimler and Stirling-Panhard. As early as 1896 he had driven from Hamilton to Carlisle and back, a distance of 167 miles which he completed in twelve hours. He later drove from Edinburgh to London in two days.

A Stirling bus, produced at the former Madelvic Works at Granton, Edinburgh around 1902.
© Glasgow Museums

Stirling Motor Carriages built mainly to order, without a standard model of its own. John Stirling acquired the former Madelvic premises and moved part of his assembly plant to Granton. The best known product to emerge from there was the Pioneer bus but the whole company lasted until only 1907.

The building of motor cars, however, was not confined to the central belt of Scotland. By 1899, the **Caledonian** Cycle and Motor Company of Aberdeen was making its Caledonian car at 265 Union Street, in the city centre. Engines like Daimler were brought north but the chassis were made in

1895

George Johnston's first Scottish car and the Mo-Car Syndicate is formed.

The Caledonian Motor Car and Cycle Company, Union Street, and Langstane Place, Aberdeen, of which Mr J H Paterson is the managing director, have taken up the motor business in a most energetic manner, and not only can turn out Caledonia motor vehicles of a number of different patterns including wagonette, parcel van, dog cart, and tricycle, but what is more can deliver within six weeks from date of order.
Motor World - November 1899

The Greenock authorities are determined to stand no nonsense especially from a person in charge of a motor car! They are naturally opposed to motor cars a feeling which is known to exist in more places than Greenock.
Motor World - October 1902

1920

The English branch of France's Bleriot revealed an 8hp cyclecar, the Whippet.

Aberdeen and a four-seater dog-cart became popular on the market for £200. Numbers were never large and production ended in 1906.

John Tavendale, a millwright in Laurencekirk, turned from making bicycles to cars, building his **St Laurence** model between 1895 and 1902. Tavendale made the engines himself, from castings brought up from Coventry, but he built in small numbers and eventually settled down to no more than running an ordinary garage business.

Dunfermline was the location of an interesting vehicle, the **Tod** three-wheeler, made in 1897 by Michael Tod and Sons and rather resembling the invalid carriage of later times.

1897 Tod
© Glasgow Museums

For a few years at the turn of the century John Simpson of Stirling was making a steam car, with the chassis sprung on the axles and the body sprung on the chassis. The 6-hp engine burned paraffin. Simpson followed this with a large six-seater of the dog-cart design.

Meanwhile, George Johnston, founder of the Arrol-Johnston who had parted from the company by 1904, was back in prominence as part of the new All-British Car

Company of Bridgeton, Glasgow, commonly known as the **ABC** company. It had a capital of £250,000 and a target of more than 700 vehicles per year. It produced an open-topped double-decker bus, which was not a success, and the car exhibited with a large chassis in 1907 failed to find a market. The ABC company was wound up the following year with debts of £120,000.

Another bicycle-maker, William McLean of Glasgow, had some success with his **St Vincent**, both as a car and a bus, usually fitted with the Aster engine.

As well as the large Arrol-Johnston operation, Dumfries could boast another car, made by D McKay **Drummond** of the local iron works. The bodies were made to order by another local company, A C Penman, but once again it lasted only till 1908.

1907 Drummond
© Glasgow Museums

The famous **Beardmore** company, known for its engineering, shipbuilding and aeroplane manufacture, found its place in road vehicles in a number of ways. From 1919 till 1932 it made large numbers of taxis at the former Paisley

Beardmore 12/30 Tourer
© Glasgow Museums

Beardmore Taxi
© Glasgow Museums

works of Arrol-Johnston. During the 1920s Beardmore was also making cars at Anniesland, Glasgow, both vehicles using the engines they had developed for their airship starter-motors. Between 1922 and 1935 there was also a series of diesel engines and chassis for commercial vehicles being made at Dalmuir.

Wishaw could claim the **Belhaven**, first produced experimentally as a steam car in 1906 by its parent company, Robert Morton and Sons. Taxi-cabs were the first serious production but the Belhaven name then went into heavier vehicles, lorries and charabancs, with customers like Walter Alexander, who ran the big bus company. Large numbers of lorries were turned out during the First World War but the company closed down in 1924.

Another significant name to enter the scene was that of Walter Bergius of Glasgow, a former engineering apprentice at Weir's of Cathcart who set up his own motor manufacturing business in 1904, when he was still in his early twenties.

Again, he acquired part of the premises at Finnieston Street which had been used by both Albion and Halley and the car he produced was the **Kelvin**, a four-seater with a rear entrance like a buggy. Most cars of the time were chain-driven but the Kelvin had a live back axle driven by a cardan shaft. The body was re-designed as a side-entrance tourer but financial difficulties arose.

In 1906 Walter's brother William suggested they might fit an engine to a rowing boat he had bought. This was the shrewd turning point for the Bergius family. The Kelvin car was soon gone but the Kelvin marine engine had just started on its road to success.

So the romance of the motor car went on, sometimes on the smallest of scales yet always indicative of the ingenuity

A 1910 Belhaven lorry built in Wishaw by Robert Morton & Sons for W W Walker. Speed limited to 12 mph!
© Glasgow Museums

1905 Kelvin built by the Bergius Car & Engine Company, Glasgow
© Glasgow Museums

1922
"Austin Seven, the car for the common man". Aimed at impoverished motor-cycle owners, the Seven boasted a 4-cylinder engine and 4-wheel brakes – a real car in miniature, claiming 75 mpg at 25 mph!

which was to be found among engineering people.

It is interesting to trace some of the other names which appeared on Scots-made cars in those pioneering days:

Atholl (1907-08): A dozen of these 25-hp cars were made by Angus Murray of Craigton Engineering, Glasgow.

Bon-Car (1905-07): A small number of steam cars made by the Edinburgh and Leith Engineering Co of Pirrie Street, Leith.

Caledon (1915-24): A wartime factory at Duke Street, Glasgow, Caledon became Scottish Commercial Cars Ltd and made buses and lorries with the Burt sleeve-valve engines. It was associated with Commer.

Caledonian (1912-14): Another company formed by the same William Peck of Madelvic, to build taxis. It took over his former works at Granton but was short-lived.

Carlaw (1920): David Carlaw & Sons (later Carlaw Cars Ltd) made a brief foray into manufacture and built three small commercial vehicles in 1920. The concession was then sold to Harper-Bean of Dudley.

Cassell (1900-03): A range of four private car models was made in limited numbers by the Central Motor Company of 111 Bothwell Street, Glasgow.

Clyde (1913-32): These were mainly lorries made by McKay and Jardine of Main Street, Wishaw. The Clyde survived longer than most, with a steady output of two vehicles per month until 1932.

Dalgleish-Gullane (1907): A Mr Dalgleish of Gullane, East Lothian, built ten cars, which were really de Dions rebuilt and improved.

DLM (1915-20): The D L Motor company of Toll Street,

Motherwell, was formed to build lorries for the First World War. Afterwards it teamed up with John Wallace of Glasgow and bought the patents for the Burt-McCollum engine, which was fitted to the Wallace and the Glasgow agricultural tractor which were also made in Scotland.

Galloway (1921-28): This was a car built first at Tongland,

1924 Galloway 12/30 hp Tourer
© Glasgow Museums

Kirkcudbright, as a subsidiary of Arrol-Johnston, and later at that company's main plant in Dumfries.

Gilchrist (1921-23): Gilchrist Cars Ltd had a small works at Giffnock, a district on the south side of Glasgow, where it built a number of cars with 11.9 Hotchkiss engines.

Grampian (1908): Grampian Engineering of Stirling embarked on an experiment with steam and motor lorries but the venture soon failed.

Harper (1898-1900): John Harper and his sons of 43 Holburn Street, Aberdeen, made primitive experimental cars of the

1908 Atholl 25 hp car chassis
© Glasgow Museums

A 1912 Ford advertisement

'tractor' type, using Benz or Cannstadt-Daimler engines.

Kennedy (1907-10 and 1921-26): Hugh Kennedy of Glasgow first made cars under the name of Kennedy and Ailsa. By 1921 he had moved to a new works in Shettleston and had made an 8-hp engine. Kennedy then went on to build his Rob Roy, which began as a two-seater coupe and was followed by larger models.

Kingsburgh (1901-02): A group of businessmen formed the Kingsburgh Motor Construction Co to begin the manufacture of cars – and gave Scotland its first purpose-built factory in that industry. By April 1902, however, the company had been sold to Stirling Motor Carriages.

Knightswood (1914): This was a three-wheeler car made in the west end of Glasgow.

Lambert (1914): This was a cycle car made by Leslie Lambert of Drumchapel, Glasgow. Only one appears to have been made – and it was amphibious!

Lothian (1915-25): While many bus operators assembled buses on chassis of another make, Scottish Omnibuses (SMT) in Edinburgh built some complete chassis for their own use and to sell to other companies for buses and lorries.

Milton (1920-21): About 20 Miltons were made by the Belford Motor Co of Edinburgh, all fitted with Dorman engines.

Ridley (1901-07): John Ridley of George Place, Paisley, made this model both as a two-seater and as a van. The Ridley Autocar Co later moved to Coventry.

Scotia (1905): A small company in Springfield Road, Glasgow, built commercial vehicles under this name.

Scotsman (1922-23): A dozen light cars were made by the Scotsman Motor Car Co of Wigton Street, Glasgow, but had no connection with another of the same name.

Scotsman (Sara) 1929-30: Another Scotsman company, of Gorgie, Edinburgh, built cars fitted with French 'Sara' engines and later with the 'Meadows' make. The Sara Scotsman became known as the Little Scotsman.

Seetstu (1906-07): This small car with the eccentric name, thought to have been a three-wheeler, was made by James McGeoch of Incle Street, Paisley.

Sentinel (1904-15): This was a steam lorry built in considerable numbers by Alley and MacLellan, Glasgow

1928 ARROL-ASTER STRAIGHT 8   *By Courtesy of "The Autocar."*

1928 Arrol-Aster Straight 8
© Glasgow Museums

engineers and shipbuilders.

Simpson (1897-1904): This steam car, mostly with dog-cart bodies, was made by John Simpson of Whins of Milton, Stirling.

Skeoch (1921): This very light car, with one-cylinder engine, was made by J B Skeoch (once of the Belhaven) at the

1898 Simpson car
© Glasgow Museums

At the Glasgow International Exhibition to be held next year it is intended to make a special feature of the automobile section. The executive are endeavouring to obtain the assistance of the principal manufacturers particularly the British makers. The Lord Provost interviewed the Automobile Club with a view of enlisting its patronage.
Motor World - May 1900

1924
J G Parry-Thomas achieved 109 mph in his Leyland-Thomas, a new world record.
In a booming market for accessories, new "Wilson" driving goggles claimed an advance in safety, boasting "unsplinterable" Triplex glass.

Burnside Motor Works in Dalbeattie. About eight of them were produced, selling at £165-£180, before the factory was destroyed by fire.

Stewart-Thorneycroft (1902-15): Duncan Stewart and Co, a Glasgow engineering company, formed a subsidiary in Bridgeton to make steam lorries with Thorneycroft engines. Sizeable numbers were produced.

Unitas (early 1920s): A chassis with special radiators was supplied by the Belhaven company to the Scottish Wholesale Cooperative Society, which mounted its own bodies and used the finished vehicles within their own business. United Cooperative Baking Society also used them.

Victoria (1906-07): This was a rebuilt and modified version of a Peugeot and a Chenard Walker, made by the Victoria (Peacock) and Autocar Co of the Craigpark Works in Dennistoun, Glasgow.

Waverley (1901-04): A dozen or so of this model were made by the Scottish Motor Company, a subsidiary of the New Rossleigh Motor and Cycle Co of Leith Walk, Edinburgh.

Werbell (1907-09): This model was made in Dundee by William and Edward Raikes Bell. It had a 25-hp White and Poppe engine and sold for £520.

1921 Skeoch car
© Glasgow Museums

A Dalhousie two-seater, manufactured by The Anderson-Grice Company Ltd of Carnoustie about 1907
© George Oliver Archive

Mr Alexander Winton the head of the large and important American automobile company bearing his name and who is at present in this country is to be married to Miss La Belle McGlashan of Paisley on Tuesday next. Although a naturalised American, Mr Winton is a true Scot and it is appropriate that he should choose a Scottish lady for his bride and be married in his native country. We extend to the couple our heartiest good wishes.
Motor World - 9 December 1905

The first use of a motor car at a wedding ceremony in Scotland. Mr E J Robertson Grant, the well known holder of the Lands End to John O' Groats motor car record was married on the 6th December to Miss Margaret Waddell of Edinburgh.
Motor World - 16 December 1905

1925
Rolls-Royce's Phantom 40/50 was in world-wide demand, especially from the Indian aristocracy, who found it suited their hunting needs. The Kumar of Viziangaram had a "huge net arranged on the near-side running board large enough to accommodate two dead tigers".

The Great Pioneers

ALEXANDER GOVAN

Except for a cruel twist of fate, Alexander Govan might well have been Scotland's answer to Henry Ford, such was the extent of his visionary ambition.

He was born at Blantyre in 1869, a weaver's son who served his apprenticeship as a mechanic in a weaving factory in Bridgeton, Glasgow, and attended evening classes at the Glasgow and West of Scotland Technical College, where he won a medal for engineering design.

As a very young man he went into business with his brother-in-law, John Worton, in Bridgeton's Bain Street, making a bicycle called the Worvan, combining their names. But the venture didn't succeed and Govan went off to seek more experience of the cycle industry in England.

On returning to Glasgow, he was caught up in the excitement over the motor car, which was about to go into commercial production in Scotland, through the enterprise of that other pioneer, George Johnston.

Keen to be involved in this industry of the future, Govan gained the financial backing of William Alexander Smith, a prosperous Glasgow merchant with many business ramifications. Smith owned a failed cycle factory in Hozier Street, Bridgeton, and it was there that they launched the venture which led to car assembly.

In 1899 Alexander Govan produced his Argyll Voiturette, which was modelled on the Renault. The subsequent development of that enterprise, with the move to a palatial new building at Alexandria, in the Vale of Leven, is told in the chapter about the Argyll car company, at one stage producing more cars than anyone in Europe.

Only Henry Ford in America was in a bigger way and Govan had been to the United States to see what intelligence he could gather. The prospect of a Scot at that level was shattered, however, by the tragic end of this young visionary when he was still in his thirties.

His death followed a meal at the old Grosvenor Restaurant in Glasgow and was at first put down to food poisoning, though the issue was confused by evidence of a cerebral haemorrhage.

Govan's early death in 1907 was to have serious consequences for the whole Argyll venture. For a man of such drive and initiative he was rather a private person, described in his obituary as "a striking although far from obtrusive figure in industrial circles in the West of Scotland."

GEORGE JOHNSTON

George Johnston is generally credited with being the father of the motor car in Scotland. Certainly he imported a Panhard towards the end of 1895 and was soon designing his own vehicle.

For Johnston was basically an inventor, an engineer of great skill, though he came from the unlikely background of the manse at Springburn, Glasgow, where his father was the United Presbyterian minister.

In that part of the city it was natural to become a locomotive engineer but soon after his training he was spreading his inventions towards various industries, including a machine for making pandrops, a sweet well known in those days as a timer of ministers' sermons!

Glasgow Corporation commissioned him to produce a steam tramcar but it was the motor car which was now his fascination. With the financial backing of Sir William Arrol, the prominent Glasgow engineer, he went into production in a company which eventually took on the name of Arrol-Johnston.

The original works in the Camlachie district of Glasgow was destroyed by fire and the company moved to Paisley, a story more fully explained elsewhere.

By 1904, however, George Johnston, a not untypical engineer more interested in machines than money, had been edged out of the business which owed so much to his inspiration.

The story of Arrol-Johnston took its own course while the founder tried to start another company for the production of

Alexander Govan 1869 – 1907
© Mitchell Library

Burberrys advert in the Motor-Car World, May 1900

1926
The Gothenburg Volvo firm built a new, mass-production factory to make cars, although just 297 were produced in the first year.

cars and buses. Before it was properly in business, however, it was taken over by the All British Car Company of Bridgeton, which set a target of 750 vehicles per year. Lord Rosebery's family were involved as directors but that ambitious venture failed in 1908, winding up with a deficit of £120,000.

That was when George Johnston disappeared from the Scottish scene altogether. His inventive streak was now working on mining machinery and was next to be found in Mexico where he managed the West Mexican Mines Ltd from 1908 until 1926.

With his lack of interest in material matters, Johnston never did make money and needed some family support in later years.

In an age when we take the motor car for granted, it was fascinating to read, as recently as 1966, an account of Johnston taking delivery of that first model. His nephew, Robert Thomson, wrote a letter to the Glasgow Herald recalling that his uncle had to learn first of all how to start the thing and then how to control it.

He was given permission to use the carriageway of Springburn Park after closing time, as the first person in Scotland trying to master the art of driving a car.

A witness to Johnston's arrival on the public highway was that other pioneer of motoring, R J Smith, who was secretary of the Royal Scottish Automobile Club for 43 years. At a dinner in 1939 he gave his audience this first-hand account: "I well remember driving with George Johnston in his car through the streets of Glasgow – and the amazement and excitement of the public at the presence of the first car seen here."

It was left to others to piece his story together, though Johnston himself was actually still alive when R J Smith gave his recollections.

In fact he quietly re-appeared to watch an old-car rally at the Empire Exhibition at Bellahouston Park, Glasgow, in 1938. Nowadays his significance to Scotland's motor car industry would have made him the subject of major interviews, with appearances on television - and perhaps some kind of public recognition even if this country is rather notorious for neglecting her illustrious.

In a vastly different age George Johnston - he never married - just melted away and died in Edinburgh in 1945 at the age of 90. But surely he will forever be associated with the start of the motor car in Scotland - and the elegance of those models which carried his name.

T C PULLINGER

If George Johnston was the engineering genius who launched the Scottish motor car industry, the Arrol-Johnston company which bore his name had to look elsewhere to find business stability.

It was in 1909, five years after the founder's departure, that Thomas Charles Pullinger came to Paisley to give Arrol-Johnston the direction it needed and to prove himself a worthy pioneer of motor production in Scotland, both as a manager and designer.

Pullinger was born within the sound of Bow Bells, son of a paymaster in Queen Victoria's Navy, and had early experience of Scotland when his family lived in Rothesay.

They moved back south and, due to family misfortune, he left school early, became a draughtsman at the Woolwich Arsenal and caused a stir when he arrived with the first bicycle seen inside the premises. Intrigued by the contraption, he went to work for the company which invented the oil-bath chain-case and then started making bicycles himself. He also began to race on the machines and became a champion in the sport.

The enterprising Pullinger was then off to Paris, working as a designer with the Darracq company but returned as manager of Sunbeam, where he turned a heavy loss into a profit and designed the 12hp Sunbeam car with chain drive (chains enclosed in Carter gear cases), the first car to be so equipped.

He moved to Humber before heading north to join Arrol-

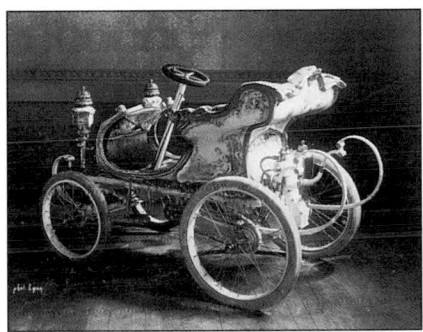

This amazing little vehicle known as "La Mouche" was built by Pullinger in 1900 for the Sultan of Turkey
Photo courtesy Yvette Le Couvey

Pullinger, seen here bringing the first motor bicycle to enter Paris in 1894 attracting huge crowds
Photo courtesy Yvette Le Couvey

1927
Triumph expanded its range with the Super Seven, a serious rival for Austin. The Model A appeared as a rugged and simple Ford Model T replacement.

Johnston at Paisley, where he was soon appointed managing director and part-owner with William Beardmore.

The Paisley works were too small, however, and Pullinger was the force behind the move to Dumfries, giving that town the taste of being a major car producer.

During the First World War Pullinger designed the Beardmore aircraft engine and was awarded the CBE. He

Thomas C Pullinger CBE JP
Picture courtesy Yvette Le Couvey

retired through ill health in 1926 and went to live in Jersey. And the man who so extended the life of Arrol-Johnston died in South Kensington, London, in 1945.

THOMAS BLACKWOOD MURRAY

Of all the pioneering figures in Scotland's automobile industry there was none more outstanding than Thomas Blackwood Murray, co-founder and main inspiration of Albion Motors, the most enduring of all the companies.

Murray was himself the son of an unusual man, John Lamb Murray, farmer at Heavyside, Biggar, who was also a self-taught architect and engineer of distinction, specialising in the design of electric light and water power installations. Keen on music, he also built a large organ which he installed in the house at Heavyside, powering it from his own dam.

Thomas was just five when his mother died so he became all the more immersed in his father's inventions, acquiring his own reputation for mending the clocks of the district while still a child.

After school in Biggar and at George Watson's College, he had already graduated from Edinburgh University as a B.Sc in engineering by the age of nineteen. In that same year he patented a water turbine speed governor which was to have a worldwide sale and he was soon in business as a consultant engineer, as well as managing the installations of Mavor and Coulsons, the prominent Glasgow engineering company.

When motor car fever hit Scotland in the mid - 1890s Murray joined George Johnston in the Mo-Car Syndicate which became Arrol-Johnston, along with Norman Fulton, who was Johnston's cousin.

Rather frustrated with Johnston's ways, those were the two men who broke away to form Albion Motors, backed financially by Murray's father, who mortgaged Heavyside for the purpose. He also bought their first engine to power his electricity system - and had a hand in the fact that many of

Dr Thomas Blackwood Murray
DSc, MInsCE, FRAeS, JP
1871 – 1929
Courtesy of Diana Blackwood Murray

Albion's early customers came from the Biggar district.

They were buying those first dog-carts which were thought to be better suited to the Scottish roads than the voiturettes.

Production moved from the original site in Finnieston Street, Glasgow, to a factory at nearby Scotstoun. By now Murray and Fulton were adding lorries to their production and building up an export trade as far away as India, New Zealand and Australia.

With the First World War, Albion were turning out thousands of three-ton vehicles for the War Office and, in spite of indifferent health, Murray made several visits to the front. In that war, he also turned his hand to the design of aero-engines which were being built by the Beardmore company at the ice-rink at Crossmyloof, on the south side of Glasgow.

Murray was a fairly autocratic figure but his skill and foresight were beyond doubt. For example, in an address to engineers and shipbuilders in 1919 he spoke of the need to be thinking of new road systems, with dual-carriageways and bridged intersections, and prophesied the end of the tramways.

Outwith his business routine, T Blackwood Murray ran a Sunday School at Biggar Kirk and became the youngest Master Mason in Scotland. As was common at the time, tuberculosis had claimed his mother and one sister and he too was affected by 1913.

In search of a better climate he bought an estate in Hampshire, to which he took the famous organ from Heavyside, both for his own love of music and for the memory of his father.

But the TB worsened and he moved to Switzerland, fighting the disease with great will-power. He kept his position as chairman of Albion until just before his death in 1929, when he was 58.

What more appropriate than that his body was finally taken to Biggar Kirk on board an Albion three-tonner?

Messers Wylie & Lochhead Ltd, the well known Glasgow cab hirers, have ordered 16 hp cab chassis from the Albion Company for hiring purposes. The bodies of the landaulette type will be built by Wylie & Lochhead with seats for four plus two extra seats beside the driver. The vehicles will be able to be hired by the hour or afternoon as desired.
Motor World - 7 May 1908

Dr Havelock, physician superintendent of Montrose Royal Lunatic Asylum, stated in his annual report that two persons had succumbed to a new disorder known as "motor mania", a condition said to be induced by the strain of driving mechanically propelled vehicles on the road. We wonder how many people have gone mad for less strains than this?
Motor World - 24 June 1905

1929
At Le Mans Bentleys came 1-2-3-4, Wolf/ Birkin's 6.5 litre leading the other three 4.5s to a beautifully choreographed finish in front of the grandstand.

JAMES ANDERSON

Through a mutual friend, I was once invited to spend a social evening at the home of James Anderson of Newton Mearns and found myself intrigued by one gadget after another.

It was clear I was in the company of an inventive genius and, with his passion for the cine-camera, it meant that whatever he created he also filmed. As he switched on the projector you would be transported to the magnificent scenery in the Land of the Midnight Sun - with camera fixed to the car so that James Anderson could film while he drove.

It was not until later, however, that I fully realised the significance of this modest bachelor who wrote himself into motoring history by building four remarkable vehicles, the "Anderson Specials," between the wars.

In his improvisation, he designed his own machine tools which turned out to be superior to those being used by the big manufacturers. At the family garage, for example, he invented a highly versatile lathe which he called the Vertimax and which was taken up by Goodyear and Lockheed to produce their disc brakes.

This was such an important development that he moved into production of the

James Anderson
© Glasgow Museums

Vertimax in a nearby factory at Spiersbridge. He eventually sold that out to Charles Churchill of Birmingham but he would wryly tell his visitor of massive orders from the United States for which he was still receiving royalties.

After the Second World War his inventions included the machine taken up by the Ford Company of America to make their exhaust manifolds. Ford bought the patent and James Anderson moved on to his next ingenious thought.

But it was the four special cars which caught the general public's imagination. And it all began in a family business which started as a cycle shop which his father, Robert Anderson, ran in Thornliebank, Glasgow.

From there to a garage on the green fields of Newton Mearns, on the southern rim of Glasgow, and he was joined by three of his sons, James, Robert and Maurice. A fourth son, John, became an academic, the much-remembered headmaster of Woodfarm and Eastwood Schools.

The first of James Anderson's specials, produced in the early 1920s, came after he developed his own welding equipment and was unique in having a lightweight welded chassis/body-frame.

The Andersons were said to be the oldest Humber agency in the world so James used an 8/18 Humber engine and gearbox. For the benefit of the technically-minded, what made his car different was the ingenuity of splitting the prop shaft and installing a bearing midway to cut down vibration. With his chassis/body-frame he was able to weld a smooth underside to the car and he achieved a top speed of 70mph, or 20mph faster than the original car from which the engine came.

Still in the 1920s, Anderson's Mark II was a sensation in its day and can still be seen in Glasgow Transport Museum. Even though he claimed 100mph on an early run out by Malletsheugh, he was dissatisfied and scrapped the engine. People were intrigued by his flat-eight engine mounted in the rear with a tapering shape, and the front track wider than the rear.

Among its novelties the Mark II had its speedometer on

1930
The 1930 Road Traffic Act ushered in many rules that still define British motoring today. Third party insurance and a declaration of physical fitness, particularly eyesight, for a licence were now mandatory. The minimum age for car drivers was now 17 and "driving without due care and attention" became an offence; "dangerous driving" now meant a £50 fine. But the 20 mph speed limit on cars was axed.

The Anderson Special at Killoure Hill, Girvan, March 1936.
Premier award winner in the 1500cc plus class
© Glasgow Museums

the end of the bonnet and, whereas the car seemed to have no headlights, Anderson surprised you by turning a handle and swivelling them out from the side of the bonnet!

The Mark III was another winner but the Mark IV was most famous of all, designed as the ultimate in trials cars and so invincible that it was often blamed for the demise of trials in Scotland. The formula was changed to ban four-wheel drive.

With the Mark IV, Anderson was said to be 25 years ahead of his time, since the basis of his suspension was a rubber and hydraulic combination. To prove its exquisite design, he would remove one wheel and drive round in circles on three wheels! He eventually gave its skeleton to some Rover Scouts.

James Anderson himself would drive off on memorable adventures, once having acquired Stirling Moss's Sunbeam Alpine, sailed to Russia and then driven all the way back

alone, crossing the Finnmark Plateau without seeing a soul for seven hours (He had fitted a 25-gallon fuel tank).

Such was the man in whose company I spent a memorable evening in the 1960s. Anderson's of Newton Mearns went out of business in 1980 but James was long retired by then. He ended his days at the local Wellmeadow retirement home where he died in 1990, at the age of 90 - the last of a pioneering breed from those early days of motoring.

The 'Anderson Special' of the mid-1930s.
A unique vehicle made in Newton Mearns.
© Glasgow Museums

Model 'T' Conquers Ben Nevis

It would be regarded as a crazy adventure even towards the end of the 20th century. So imagine the public reaction in 1911 when Henry Alexander of Edinburgh announced that he was planning to drive his 20hp Ford car right to the top of Ben Nevis. Britain's highest mountain? Surely this was a fantasy trip.

Alexander set out to prove it otherwise. As a son of the Alexander family of Leith – a name still prominent in car distribution today – Henry was caught up in the enthusiasm of their new-found dealership.

The Alexanders ran cinemas and dance halls in Edinburgh and now, in another branch of their enterprise, they had the Ford car to sell. What a publicity stunt it would be if Henry could achieve his ambition.

Mr P L D Perry, a senior official of the Ford Motor Company, was so interested in the idea that he accompanied Alexander to Fort William to explore the mountain and assess the feasibility. Early examination was not encouraging but an exploration of the north-eastern side of Ben Nevis, from the Long John Distillery to the Half-Way House, offered a ray of hope.

It was clear that the first 1000ft would present major difficulties, like the raging mountain torrents, massive boulders and treacherous bogland. But Henry Alexander decided to have a go, starting from a farmhouse on the Spean Bridge road, a few miles east of Fort William. On May 9, 1911, he set out on the five-and-a-half-mile climb to the Half-Way House, a route of rock-strewn moorland, heath-clad bog and water courses.

Slowly but surely be bumped his way up Ben Nevis, aided by a team of workmen whose job it was to clear the boulders, blast obstructing rocks and lay planks across a stream or marshy ground. At the end of each day's toil, the car was left on the mountainside under tarpaulin, awaiting Alexander's return next morning.

At last the Half-Way House was reached and the rest of the journey would be by the pony-track, a rough path about four feet wide. The gradients now became steeper and so

narrow and dangerous at some bends that the Ford had to be lifted round by the workmen. At 3000ft the track wound in zig-zag fashion along the upper ridges, with snow lying four feet deep.

At that stage, Alexander confessed he didn't expect to reach the top. With sheer determination, however, he kept rushing at the gradients and reached the table-land of snow, leaving the last 400ft to be tackled on a newly-created track because of its depth.

A final surge and he was there! One of the greatest achievements in the history of motoring, even now, had been accomplished. The ascent had taken five-and-a-half days, with no mechanical adjustments and under the car's own power, except for those helping hands at hair-pin bends.

Back down south, Mr Perry hastily arranged for a train-load of journalists to travel north to witness this amazing feat with their own eyes. They arrived at Fort William and started out for Britain's highest point, following precisely the route taken by Alexander.

Neil Munro was to write that those journalists were "culled like innocent flowers from the London sleeping-car and heaved upon horseback without a moment's opportunity to acquaint themselves with the magnitude of the task. As if with crafty purpose to conceal from them the appalling bulk of the Ben until they were too far advanced to retreat from the adventure, the squadron of unsuspecting English gentlemen was led up a corrie from which the white forehead and fierce escarpment of the mountain was screened."

Munro continued: "A little later and the shameless iniquity

Henry Alexander in his Model 'T' Ford at the summit
© Mitchell Library

of Mr Perry's tactics was revealed. Ben Nevis, aloof, august, apparently unconquerable, smiled derisively upon the straggling cavalcade, now experiencing discomforts novel to the motor journalist which, I take it, is mostly done on well-sprung cushions."

One Fleet Street man was caught by the top wire of a deer-fence and left dangling like a scarecrow as his horse went flying from under him.

In time the place was like a battlefield, Mr Gray of the Motor World magazine falling nastily to smash his tooth and bite his tongue!

The comedy continued till, at last, they caught sight of the summit – and there stood Alexander's Ford car, "complacent and self-satisfied and apparently ready for further calls upon its resources," as one observer said. It didn't seem to have a scratch on it.

The scene at the top of Ben Nevis was without parallel. Pedestrians and equestrians bustled around for eatables and drinkables, photographers and cinematographers hustled the journalists into groups to record this moment in history and the normally pampered pressmen of Fleet Street drew breath to take in the magnificent view of the Cairngorms to the east, Ben More and Ben Lawers to the south and the sunlit Hebrides to the west and north.

But soon it was time for the descent, which would prove that this had been no hoax. In the event, most of the journalists had difficulty finding words to describe this remarkable performance of man and car.

With astounding nonchalance, and with cameras trained upon him, Henry Alexander took off on that downward journey, petrifying the journalists by bouncing over boulders and through waterfalls as they struggled to find footholds for themselves while trying to absorb the spectacle of a lifetime.

As one observer wrote: "Looked at from in front, the car seemed literally to leap towards you; from behind, to jump and bump and hurl itself from one boulder to another. The brakes, springing, steering wheel and the entire mechanism worked in one fine harmonious whole, while the man sat

easily at his gigantic task – all unconscious of the sudden shocks and nerve-shattering sensations which we vainly endeavoured to control."

As Alexander negotiated the narrow bridge over the Red Burn and crossed the tumbling mountain torrent, the journalists gave vent to their pent-up emotions with a ringing cheer which echoed into the glen below.

On arrival at the Distillery, examination of the car showed that not a bolt or screw was loose, the engine ran as quietly and sweetly as it did before the ordeal – and Alexander felt as fit as a fiddle.

The whole of Fort William, headed by a pipe band, marched out to meet him as he returned to the town. The Lion Rampant, torn and tattered by the winds of the Ben, fluttered bravely from the back of the Ford, while the Stars and Stripes of its home country adorned the radiator.

Alexander was carried shoulder-high into the Caledonian Hotel, where there were speeches and celebrations.

As word of the incomparable feat circled the world, Henry Ford counted his saving from a welter of free publicity and remarked that he wouldn't need to spend a single dime on promotion that year!

Footnote:
Vehicles have been driven up Ben Nevis on four occasions. George Simpson in an Austin 7 in 1928, Henry Alexander (twice) in 1911 and 1928. The most recent ascent was in 1987 by two Suzuki ATV Quad Runners from Old Inverlochy Castle in a time of 2 hours 21 minutes.

Negotiating the equally tricky descent of the mountain
© Mitchell Library

The first ever British lorry to change over to giant pneumatic tyres is one currently in service in Glasgow. The conversion to "Nobby Cord" tyres was made by Messers Stevenson & Co of Glasgow.
Motor World - March 1920

1933
The London to Baghdad train service is now linked by a Rolls-Royce shuttle for the 250 miles separating Turkey's and Iraq's railheads.

Rootes at Linwood

The mass ownership of the motor car in Britain really began to take shape in the 1950s, as the world emerged from the bruising of the Second World War and looked towards better economic times.

In planning to meet the demand, the manufacturing companies found themselves directed by government incentive to build factories in areas of high unemployment rather than in locations which would have suited their own convenience. Ford, Vauxhall and Standard-Triumph, for example, went to Merseyside.

The Rootes Group had plans to create a new small car, which became known as the Hillman Imp, and a new factory was needed outwith the existing capacity. The choice would have been a site within easy reach of the home base at Coventry but the government had other ideas.

In September 1960 it was announced that Rootes would build a factory at Linwood in Renfrewshire, 10 miles west of Glasgow. There were certain advantages in this, apart from the government's financial help. It would be next door to the Pressed Steel factory which already made bodies for Rover and Volvo and would provide a natural service for Rootes.

In 1958, Colville's had set up a steel strip mill at Ravenscraig in Lanarkshire, again a ready-made source of materials. And finally, with the decline of shipbuilding on the Clyde, there would be a plentiful supply of labour.

There was, of course, one glaring disadvantage. While the block and cylinder head for the engine of the new car would be made at Linwood, it would all have to be transported to the main plant at Coventry to be fitted to the rest of the engine – and sent back to Linwood for final assembly. With a round trip of 600 miles, it was not a model of economic sense.

For Renfrewshire, however, it was an enormous boost, requiring new houses, schools and shopping centres and better road and rail links.

The new £24 million factory was opened by the Duke of Edinburgh at a lavish ceremony in May 1963, attended by such diverse personalities of the day as the Rootes family,

Official opening – The Duke of Edinburgh with Geoffrey Rootes look at a completed engine assembly
© The Herald

The first Imp to leave the production line at Linwood now displayed in Glasgow's Museum of Transport
© The Herald

The Linwood factory complex
© The Herald

newspaper tycoon Roy Thomson, union leader Frank Cousins, the Duke of Hamilton, Sir William Lithgow, Cameron of Lochiel and Liberal leader Jo Grimond, as well as Dr Beeching, the man engaged to cut the heart out of Britain's rural railways.

An immediate workforce of 3000 turned out 850 Hillman Imps per week, which was less than a third of capacity. But problems were soon building up. The Rootes company, which had already been losing money, was soon to come under the control, of the Chrysler company of America.

Then the Hillman Imp, which was not a cheap car to build, had technical problems which gave it a mixed reputation. We were also in the age of the labour disputes which were giving Britain a bad name abroad.

So the sales of the Imp were disappointing and production of the Hillman Hunter medium range was moved from Coventry to Linwood, with a further £20 million spent on the factory.

Linwood reached its peak in 1972 when it was turning out 2400 cars a week. It was also making body panels for assembly at Coventry and overseas - and there were nine trains a week carrying 3500 gearboxes and 3700 rear axles and front suspensions and steering arms to Coventry for the Avenger.

But the oil crisis of the 1970s brought further trouble to Chrysler, calling for more government aid. Drastic decisions had to be made. The Imp was to be dropped altogether and the Avenger transferred from Coventry to Linwood, where they would also build another new car, the Sunbeam.

The workforce reached a substantial 8400 and, with weekly production targets of 1750 Avengers and 1050 Sunbeams, Linwood had become the main part of the Chrysler operation in the United Kingdom.

But targets were not met, labour troubles persisted and in 1978 the Chrysler company announced it was selling its European operation to Peugeot/Citroen of France, which brought back the famous name of Talbot.

By now the world was in recession, the car market was declining and the French company was losing ground to its keen rival, Renault. The geographical location of the Scottish plant, along with its history of industrial unrest, put it in line for closure. And what started out as such a promising venture in 1963 came to an end in 1981, by which time the workforce had been slimmed to 4800. As so often happens, the labour relations were then at their best for some time.

But the mass production of the motor car was gone, shattering an ideal and restoring the need to find, once again, a solution to the economic depression of the Paisley district.

In 1907 the 'Motor World' which was then a weekly publication could be had on subscription for one year for the sum of five shillings.
Motor World - 26 January 1907

1935
The tenacious Sir Malcolm Campbell raised his own land-speed record to 301mph in Bluebird at Utah's Bonneville Salt Flats, surviving a burst tyre at 280mph.

The Rise and Fall of Bathgate

Just as the Rootes company was directed to Linwood, bringing the mass production of the motor car to Scotland, so did the government of Harold Macmillan simultaneously guide the British Motor Corporation towards Bathgate, West Lothian, where it would provide a corresponding economic boost with its production of trucks and tractors.

This large-scale operation, which would eventually come under the name of British Leyland, rolled into action in October 1961, when the first truck was driven off the assembly line.

In less than a year it had turned out more than 9000 vehicles and, with the entire range of BMC's heavy vehicles now transferred to Bathgate, the second year saw the total rise above 28,000.

With this bustling activity close by the main Glasgow-Edinburgh road, the local authorities built more than 1000 houses, with 570 families moving from Glasgow to start life in a totally new environment.

Among the aims of directing BMC to Scotland was to provide jobs for redundant workers in the shale-oil industry which had come to an end. As the Bathgate workforce expanded from 2000 towards 6000 those ex-miners did indeed take up more than 1400 of the jobs.

Bathgate became the centre of the company's vehicle production and by 1978 three-quarters of all Leyland trucks over 3.5 tons were being produced either there or at Albion Motors in Glasgow, which was already part of the same group.

Throughout the 1960s and 1970s Bathgate was counted a highly profitable operation and there were plans for expansion which would have doubled the workforce to around 13,000. But it didn't happen. And some disturbing trends were beginning to show, including a lack of investment. There was a feeling that profits from those heavier

Finished Nuffield Tractors leaving the production line
© Glasgow Museums

BMC trucks on the production line at Bathgate
© Glasgow Museums

A light car of original design shown for the first time in Scotland at the recent Motor Show in Edinburgh was the Ford. This little car was shown in both the chassis form and complete with a 2 seated body. The frame was of pressed steel and the engine a four cylinder type with 15 horsepower being developed at normal speed. It is reckoned to offer wonderful value at £165.
Motor World - 6 April 1907

Bonnet position. In designing the modern hinged bonnet it is important that it should be arranged so as to allow one to get the screwdriver and hand-brace vertically into the valve holes for the purpose of grinding. I have seen many bonnets with the fixed position at the top just wide enough to be seriously in the way and grinding valves becomes a nuisance instead of a keen delight as it should be perhaps.
Motor World - 27 April 1907

1936
W O Bentley's influence was seen on the introduction of the great new V12 Lagonda and the Jensen brothers also revealed their first car, Ford V8 powered.

vehicles were being diverted to support the ailing car division down south.

In a competitive market where Leyland had held a comfortable lead, it was overtaken by Ford in 1977 and three years later its market share had declined even further.

It was the age of powerful unions and a critical point was reached in 1978 when Leyland was caught up in an unofficial strike. Company chairman Michael Edwardes withdrew some planned investment as a "punishment," with Bathgate bearing the brunt of the penalty. In his subsequent autobiography, Edwardes claimed his action had the blessing of the Labour Prime Minister of the day, James Callaghan.

In the late 1970s, Leyland at Bathgate had been exporting its varied range of trucks to 70 countries. By 1984 that product range had been reduced to two specialist models and the 6000 workforce had gone back to the original 2000.

There was many a post mortem on the closure which was finalised in 1986. Some fingers were pointed at the Leyland management. They in turn blamed recession. The view of most economists was that the well-meaning policy of grafting those industries on to an unreceptive host economy had, in fact, been a failure.

Thus the mass production of commercial vehicles at Bathgate was to disappear, taking with it an important element in the Scottish economy.

A general view of the BMC (Scotland) Ltd Bathgate factory from the north. The buildings covered 1.25 million square feet.

© Glasgow Museums

A motorists hotel. The Crown & Mitre Hotel, Carlisle is a house that I am never tired of recommending as an ideal motorists house. One is always welcome there and the manager is a good sort who understands motorists. There is a capital garage which one can get into without turning any awkward corners - a great thing in these days of a long wheel base.
Motor World - December 1906

Notes & News - Motor cars on Ayrshire roads. Mr Alan Stevenson, Surveyor, reported that the damage done to the roads by motor car traffic at a meeting of Ayr District Committee of the Ayr County Council last week. The traffic he said interfered with roads in several ways and caused an increased quantity of metal to be used. It was, he added, the fast traffic by motorists that was the most injurious to the roads.
Motor World - 26 January 1907

1937
The inhabitants of the Island of Barra, led by novelist Compton Mackenzie, refused to pay their road-taxes as the island's roads were so bad.

Halley's Triumph

By the time Bathgate ended, that other Scottish company in the Leyland group, the longstanding Albion Motors, had also ceased to assemble complete vehicles, though it was still a substantial supplier of components.

The Albion story, meriting a chapter of its own, dated back to the beginning of the century, when it was not the only company to see the advantage of concentrating on the commercial sector.

While still in his early twenties, the enterprising George Halley, in 1901, was producing steam lorries in an old weaving mill at Crownpoint Road, Glasgow, and preparing to challenge the Albion company with his petrol vehicles.

Halley's Industrial Motors was registered in 1906 and soon his two-ton van chassis with 20hp two-cylinder governed engine was proving a winner, for example, among Scotland's bakery firms, who were always to the fore in modern transport. By now he had moved to a spacious factory at Yoker.

Halley's vehicles were highly regarded, including his fire engines, which were much in demand with municipalities like Glasgow and there was also a 34-seater bus chassis. Their vehicles were driven by Tyler or Crossley engines as well as the ones they made themselves. Diverted to war work in 1914, the company extended its good name to the battlefields of France before returning to peacetime production as soon as possible.

In 1920 a new six-cylinder, four-speed worm-drive chassis stirred much attention as Halley set out to make it the Rolls-Royce of industrial transport. But the man himself was in failing health and he died in 1921 while still only 43 years old.

Within a few years his company was losing money and chose voluntary liquidation, surviving in a reconstructed form.

The Scottish Motor Show of 1934 saw the last of the Yoker product and George Halley's worthy enterprise suffered the irony of falling into the hands of his old rival, Albion Motors.

Having supplied the first mechanically propelled fire engine to Glasgow Corporation in 1910, it was appropriate that the last vehicle to leave the Yoker works in 1935 was a new engine for Clydebank Fire Brigade.

Halley radiator badge
© Alan Carlaw

1938
The talented German, Bernd Rosemeyer, widely known as a vital but strange personality, died when his Auto-Union swerved off course attempting a speed record on a German autobahn. Hitler wrote to his widow - "May the thought that he fell fighting for Germany's reputation lessen your grief"!

Halley B.1 2½ ton carrier's lorry well laden with trunks and other goods
© Glasgow Museums

Halley G.3 6-ton lorry used by William Milne from their cold store at 40 Old Wynd, Glasgow
© Glasgow Museums

Alexander's Buses to Stagecoach

If Halley's name barely survives in the Scottish psyche, that of Walter Alexander certainly does. For this was one of the great business romances of the century, symbolised by the famous Bluebird buses which caught public imagination from the 1930s onwards.

The original Walter Alexander was part of that astonishing breed of entrepreneur which has long been a feature of Scottish life. In 1902, at the age of 23, he opened a cycle shop in Camelon, near Falkirk, while retaining his job as a fitter in a local foundry. His son Walter was born in that same year and the young father was already gathering capital, with his sights on the motor business.

In 1913 he bought a Scottish-built, chain-driven Belhaven bus and ran a local service in Stirlingshire. By 1924 father and son were not only spreading their bus service but were now building their own vehicle bodies at Brown Street, Camelon.

In 1924 the Alexander company linked into Scottish Motor Traction (SMT), which became the holding company for an expanding group. The Alexanders opened a coachworks at Drip Road, Stirling, to build buses for the whole group, turning out around 160 bodies per annum throughout the 1930s.

These included the Bluebird coach, which first appeared in 1934 and set new standards in comfort and sleek design. It was one of the many inspired thoughts of young Walter, who envisaged the flying bird as an eye-catching symbol.

In 1928 the railway companies of LMS and LNER had bought a stake in SMT and that was to have far-reaching effects when the railways were nationalised in 1948. That stake passed into the hands of the state and a year later the SMT group decided to sell the rest of its bus business to the new British Transport Commission.

But the Alexanders decided to keep the coachbuilding as a business on its own. This opened up a wider market and, with a new purpose-built factory at Glasgow Road, Falkirk, in 1958, they were supplying fleets of municipal buses all over the country. Kits for local assembly became a feature in the

Early bus body construction at the Brown Street, Falkirk coachworks
Walter Alexander (Falkirk) Ltd

1970s and the Alexander reputation was spreading around the world.

Walter junior became a director in yet another reconstruction in 1969, when the Scottish Bus Group was formed. Meanwhile, the founding Walter, who had lived to see a phenomenal success for his Alexander's buses, had died in 1959 at the age of 80. Walter junior survived until 1979, when he was 77, and was followed in the business by his son Ronald.

1939
As war was declared in September, Britain's motorists felt the pinch. It was suggested to them by the government to rub ordinary soap in the middle of the transparent eye-piece to stop their gas-masks from steaming up while driving!

Leyland Titan 53-seat lowbridge double-decker bus
of the late 1930s
Walter Alexander (Falkirk) Ltd

One of a unique batch of 20 coaches supplied in 1961 to
Alexander (Midland) on Leyland Tiger Cub chassis
Walter Alexander (Falkirk) Ltd

The family put the coachbuilding company up for sale in 1989, however, and Walter Alexander was bought by a group of financial institutions. In 1995 it changed hands again and became part of the prosperous Mayflower Group.

In the late 1990s Alexander's remained the biggest producer of bus bodies in the United Kingdom.

But as in life itself, business is subject to peculiar cycles. Whereas the name of Alexander was for long the dominant force among bus operators in Scotland, it was overtaken in spectacular fashion by the Stagecoach company of Perth.

Started in the most modest of circumstances in the 1980s by the brother-and-sister partnership of Brian Souter and Ann Gloag, it exploded into massive proportions within a few years, operating buses not only in the United Kingdom but as far away as Africa and China.

By the mid-1990s they were responsible for upwards of 8500 buses around the world, an imaginative enterprise almost beyond comparison, putting their founding partners into a bracket among the wealthiest people in Britain.

How appropriate, however, that the Alexander name which Stagecoach has so over-shadowed has played a major part in building buses for that enterprising family from Perth which now rides high among the great names of Scotland's entrepreneurial history. Appropriate, too, that the father of Brian and Ann, Ian Souter, was once a driver on Alexander's buses.

White-coated drivers stand beside their new 1929 Leyland TS 1 Tigers
Walter Alexander (Falkirk) Ltd

A Stagecoach Bluebird leaving Perth en route for Inverness
© Thomson Print Services (Glasgow) Ltd

*Alexander bodied 'PS' type single-deck bus
for Stagecoach Ribble*
Walter Alexander (Falkirk) Ltd

*Alexander bodied 'R' type double deck bus
for Lothian Regional Transport*
Walter Alexander (Falkirk) Ltd

Volvo at Irvine

If the history of vehicle manufacture in Scotland has been less to do with sustained hope than eventual decline, there is always the heartening tale of the Volvo company and its assembly of trucks and buses at Irvine in Ayrshire.

It dates back to 1967 when a Scottish haulier, Jim McKelvie, teamed up with fellow-Scot Jim Keyden to form Ailsa Trucks Ltd and become the sole concessionaires in the United Kingdom for selling Volvo trucks and buses. The name was taken from the prominent rock of Ailsa Craig in the Firth of Clyde.

But in 1972 the company bought a former Royal Ordnance Depot in Irvine and set out to assemble the Volvos on an ambitious scale. The factory was opened in 1975 with an initial capacity for 900 vehicles per annum.

In 1977 the name was changed to Volvo Trucks (Great Britain) Ltd and the Volvo company itself took over the balance of ownership a year later.

By 1980, when capacity had risen to 1600 units a year, Irvine was supplying a third of all Volvo trucks sold in Britain and Ireland. It also gained main-plant status in 1984, with a greater level of autonomy.

In 1993 a new bus assembly hall enabled the building of 1500 chassis per annum and when it had marked up 20 years of existence, the Irvine factory could claim to have produced a total of 40,000 trucks and buses.

In 1995 the company announced a £6 million investment to boost its UK production by 60 per cent, bringing the truck capacity to 5500 per year and the bus-building to 2500.

In the modern style of labour relations, the 500 employees of the 1990s operated with maximum flexibility, switching between trucks and buses to match the customer demand.

The high standard of productivity and efficiency was in sharp contrast to those earlier days of demarcation dispute which once beset and tarnished the reputation of British industry.

Volvo Citybus
Photo courtesy Volvo

Volvo FH12 tractor unit
Photo courtesy Volvo

'Art and the Motor Lorry'
It is very unusual for a motor lorry to be identified with a Drama Company but that is quite practicable as the Arts League are using a 35hp Lancia to carry them and their props during their Scottish tour. This is the first time in the world that a lorry has been used for this kind of transport.
Motor World - October 1922

1945
The Sub-Committee on Post-War Reconstruction examined the car business, concluding that there were "too many companies, too many models, not enough standardisation of production and parts to ensure low cost, and a failure to design vehicles that could defeat competition overseas".

Motor Sport

The names of Jim Clark, Jackie Stewart and Innes Ireland trip-roared their way across the pages of motor sport history with such dramatic effect that England's Graham Hill was once prompted to say of the Scots: "There aren't many of them – but they are a damned nuisance!"

Hill's observation was still true a generation later when his own son Damon, following in his late father's footsteps in Formula One racing, found himself faced by another up-and-coming Caledonian clutch, led by David Coulthard – with the same Jackie Stewart launching himself back into the world-class limelight as mastermind of Stewart Grand Prix, fired by the massive funding of Ford.

But the on-going saga of the speeding Scots doesn't end with Formula One. What was being achieved in rallying in that earlier generation (by Andrew Cowan, another Duns farmer, like Jim Clark) was taken to spectacular heights in the 1990s by the incredible McRaes from Lanark.

Following hard on the heels of Jimmy the father, five times British champion, son Colin carried off the world championship in 1995, pursued by his own brother Alister, who had become British champion!

And in the same era, when you consider the success of people like John Cleland, the Galashiels car dealer who was still British Touring Car Champion well into his forties, you gain the full impact of a fabulous record of Scottish triumph and influence in the field of world motor sport.

Why such a small nation should have this grossly disproportionate success with fast cars will long remain a matter of theorising and discussion. Has it something to do with the reputation of the Scots as the world's finest engineers? Or perhaps the determination of a small, over-shadowed but proud nation to assert itself in areas where individual skill and character can cut a path to stardom?

Whatever the conclusions, the Scots have been taking a rather stylish interest in motor sport since the early days of the car, as can be seen from the chapter on the Royal Scottish Automobile Club.

But it was after the Second World War that the ground-

A Ford V8 competing in a Driving Test at the end of the 1938 Scottish Rally at the Empire Exhibition in Bellahouston Park, Glasgow
© RSAC

work was laid for the kind of competitive success which has elevated Scotland to the heights of motor racing in the second half of the century.

At first there was the hazard of petrol rationing, curtailing

Aberdeen & District Motor Club

Falkirk & District Motor Club

Highland Car & Motor Cycle Club

1946
British troops in Germany could buy a new Volkswagen, made under military supervision at Wolfsburg, for £160 and bring it home to Blighty.

Well known racing driver Bob Gerard in his ERA in the Snake chicane at Bo'ness Speed Hill Climb in 1948

the number of events which could be attended.

In those early years there were three major sporting clubs which had been established in the 1930s – the Scottish Sporting Car Club, the Falkirk and District Motor Club and the M G Car Club (Scottish Centre). They held events like rallies on public roads, with timed driving tests, gymkhanas and trials which involved climbing grass and rough tracks as far as they could go.

The SSCC re-started its speed hill climbs at Bo'ness in 1946 and its Highland Three Day Trial in 1949. In that same year the Royal Scottish Automobile Club brought in the Rest-and-be-Thankful speed hill climb on the old road, attracting competitors from far beyond Scotland.

The revival of the Monte Carlo Rally gave it a starting-point in Blythswood Square, Glasgow, which drew out huge crowds and became a fashionable rendezvous for those who wanted to see and be seen.

The Scottish Rally was also back in business and the

growing interest was reflected in the fact that Scottish drivers were competing successfully in the Rallyes International des Alpes and the Dutch International Tulpen Rallyes.

The momentum was gathering at clubs throughout Scotland, typified by the Lothian Car Club which started in 1948 and produced a memorable May Day Rally in 1955. In many of these events the ordinary sports and saloon cars were joined by home-built, one-off "specials," often adaptations of production cars and engines which were mostly obtained from the breakers' yards.

It was in 1950, however, that a wider public awareness of motor sport spread like wildfire across the country with the decision to adapt runways of Second World War airfields for use as racing circuits. It began at Winfield Airfield in the Borders, where an attendance of 15,000 spectators encouraged others to follow suit.

At the other end of the country, my own introduction to motor racing came at Crimond Airfield, between Peterhead

An MG TC Midget competing in the SSCC's Gymkhana at Callander in 1948

© Photo courtesy Nigel Kennedy

Kilmarnock Car Club

Lanarkshire Car Club

M.G. Car Club

1947
The car-mad Clark Gable was seen spectating at the Indianapolis 500 race which was won by the "Blue Crown Spark Plug Special".
Henry Ford – "The Wizard" sadly died.

and Fraserburgh, where I seem to remember, from the enthusiasm of my early journalism, that I was estimating the crowd at around 30,000.

Those meetings, held on a Sunday, were notable for two particular reasons. Firstly, Crimond was the little parish where the minister's daughter, Jessie Seymour Irvine, composed her famous psalm tune of that name – and the noise of those 30,000 people arriving for the motor racing brought fierce protests about the desecration of the Sabbath. It was said that Willie Russell the minister couldn't hear himself preach the sermon!

Secondly, although we didn't know it at the time, a young lad making his very first appearance on a racing circuit – and competing incognito – turned out to be none other than the future world racing champion, Jim Clark.

Another of those forays into motor racing took place at Turnberry in Ayrshire, where the Scottish Sporting Car Club laid out a 1.76-mile course on surviving runways. It may have been a brief encounter, running into trouble with the rates proposed by a district assessor, but it was not without its moments of glory.

Reg Parnell won a 20-lap sprint in the V-16 BRM, one of

Raymond Mays, a British Hill Climb Champion, in his ERA at the top hairpin bend at Rest and be Thankful Speed Hill Climb

© Photo courtesy Nigel Kennedy

its rare victories, and the great Stirling Moss came to race his C-type Jaguar at Turnberry. Liverpool garage-owner Gillie Tyrer also drove his Frazer-Nash BMW, one of the 1940 Mille Miglia cars looted from Germany in 1945!

The Scottish Motor Racing Club organised a 500cc race meeting at Kirkcaldy in 1954 and it was this club which later provided Scotland with its very best motor racing at Ingliston. That top spot was eventually taken over by Knockhill in Fife.

But Scotland really arrived on the international motor-racing scene in 1956 with the Ecurie Ecosse victory at Le Mans, all the more remarkable because it was the team's very first entry for the event.

Ecurie Ecosse had been the passion of three well-to-do amateurs, Bill Dobson, Ian Stewart and Sir James Scott-Douglas, who operated from lock-up garages at Merchiston Mews in Edinburgh.

The team, which was to gain worldwide fame, was

The Stafonak on New Logie Hill on a Falkirk & District Motor Club Trial in 1949

Photo courtesy Nigel Kennedy

Riley Car Club

Scottish Sporting Car Club

Scottish Motor Racing Club

1948
The Shah of Iran bought a Fraser-Nash High Speed sports car for running around Teheran. The 19-year old newcomer, Stirling Moss, set the fastest practice lap in the British GP 500cc support race at Silverstone.

The Mark II version of the Stafonak in a real mud bath on an observed section in the F & D Motor Club's Cadger's Trophy Trial in 1950.

Photo courtesy Nigel Kennedy

managed by David Murray and signed up distinguished names of the day like Ninian Sanderson and Ron Flockhart. It was Sanderson, the Glasgow garage-owner, who co-drove the winning Jaguar for the Scots at Le Mans in 1956. A year later Ecurie Ecosse won the 24-hour classic again, with Flockhart in the winning team this time, Sanderson coming second.

At club level, motor sport reached its heyday in the late 1950s when there would be several events every weekend at locations throughout Scotland. The drivers of those days were all-rounders, often using the same cars for different types of event, but gradually they came to specialise, so that one became a racing driver or a rallying or hill climb expert. Trials petered out in the 1960s and rallying was largely moved from public roads to the forestry routes, which were negotiated with incredible speed and skill.

The Touring Car Championships, using modified production saloons, provide spectacular racing which is highly popular at the tracks and on television. Scotland's Knockhill became one of the circuits used for the British Touring Car championship.

The smaller club events continued to have their place, providing a training ground for the big events, but many of the early post-war enthusiasts came to look back on those amateur days of the late 1940s and 1950s with a large measure of nostalgia.

Their sport had gone the way of society in general, fiercely competitive and highly commercial, with a massive back-up of sponsorship.

After the initial breakthrough of Ecurie Ecosse, it was a vet's son from the Borders, Innes Ireland, who was the first Scot to chalk up a Grand Prix victory – in the United States race at Watkins Glen in 1961. His up-and-coming Borders neighbour, Jim Clark from Chirnside, was also in the race that day, albeit having just been involved in the tragedy of the Italian Grand Prix when his car and that of Wolfgang von Trips were in contact and the resulting crash killed the

Mini Cooper 'S' of Stuart Parker and Stuart Brown in the 1969 RSAC Scottish Rally

Photo courtesy Stuart Parker

South of Scotland Car Club

The 55 Car Club

1949
Trials champion Ken Wharton with partner Joy Cooke, in a Ford Anglia was the surprise victor of Holland's first Tulip Rally where, it was reported "the Dutch took great pride in displaying the wonderful recovery their country has made from the ravages of war".

German driver and 14 spectators.

Two years later and Clark was world champion, at the start of a ten-year spell in which he and fellow-Scot Jackie Stewart would put their names on the world crown on five occasions. Sadly, by then, Jim Clark had himself been killed in 1968, in von Trips' own country at Hockenheim.

After Stewart's domination of the early Seventies, the Scottish graph dipped understandably, though there were always potential figures in the wings. Tom Walkinshaw from Prestonpans, for example, showed that he could drive his way towards British and European Touring Car championships before revealing an even greater flair as engineer and entrepreneur. He built up an empire of 30 companies in the car industry, with a turnover of £150 million, took a large stake in the Formula One Benetton

The St Andrews Sand Race meeting in 1950 with competitors awaiting the starting flag, left to right, Jim Gibbon (Girastro Rover), Gillie Tyrer (Frazer Nash-BMW), Archie Craig (Bongazoo MG Special)
Photograph courtesy Betty Craig

company and became the power behind world champion driver Michael Schumacher.

In the colourful range of characters who populate motor racing, Scotland saw one of its aristocrats, the Earl of Dumfries (later the Marquis of Bute) reach the level of Formula One under the name of Johnny Dumfries.

And proving it is not a sport dominated totally by men, the remarkable Louise Aitken-Walker, a shepherdess from Duns in the Borders, could rightly claim that Colin McRae was not exactly the first Scot to win the world rallying championship. Indeed she herself gained the women's title in 1990, paving the way for a magnificent Scottish double when the man from Lanark came through in 1995.

New names would appear, like that of Hugh McCaig, who owned the racing circuit at Ingliston, near Edinburgh, the man who made his money in open-cast mining and financed a revival of Ecurie Ecosse in the early 1980s. His faith was justified when the Scots returned to Le Mans with drivers like David Leslie, who also played a significant part in training the new crop of Scots racing drivers with their ambitions geared to the new century.

These young men included David Coulthard (he won his first Grand Prix in 1995), Dario Franchitti and Allan McNish, son of a BMW dealer from Dumfries, not far from the Twynholm base of Coulthard, whose father is a local haulage contractor.

These are just some of the names which placed Scotland tantalisingly on the brink of further success. At least they had the incentive of precedent, knowing that their ambitions could be fulfilled, if only they could show that they were made of the same stuff as the Irelands, Clarks and Stewarts, who took their Scottish skill and passion and proved that they could beat the world.

1950
The four cylinder Consul and six cylinder Zephyr ushered in full width styling for Britain's bigger Fords.

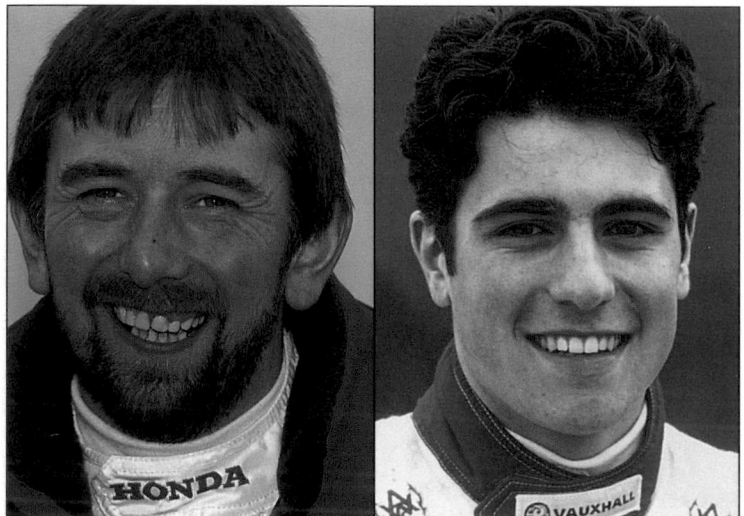

David Leslie who has followed his Formula racing career with successful participation in the British Touring Car Championship
© Autosport

Up-and-coming Bathgate born Dario Franchitti currently one of the most successful drivers in the German Touring Car Championship with Mercedes.
© The Herald

Logan Morrison and Rev Rupert Jones in a factory entered Austin-Healey finished 3rd in the Liege–Sofia–Liege Rally in 1962 and also won the manufacturers team prize

The first race meeting to be held at Turnberry Air Field was organised by the Scottish Sporting Car Club in September 1951 which was enthusiastically supported by competitors and spectators alike. Races included classes for saloon cars, sports cars, vintage sports cars, racing cars and even motor cycles.

Another meeting was held on 3 May 1952 but unfortunately the final one took place on 23 August that year when rating impositions made the holding of further events financially unviable.

The August meeting however attracted some interesting cars from south of the Border, not least the BRM driven by Reg Parnell. Stirling Moss also competed in both a 'C' Type Jaguar and a Cooper 500. Ken Wharton, the British Hill Climb champion, was forced to retire in the Formula II race when his Frazer-Nash broke a timing chain. Jimmy Stewart, brother of Jackie, also competed driving a Healey. The event was sponsored by the Scottish Daily Express and was billed as the National Trophy Race Meeting.

Reg Parnell in the BRM, winner of the Scottish National Trophy Race at Turnberry in August 1952
Top Gear

A cheerful Stirling Moss in his Cooper 500 delighted the Turnberry crowd in 1952
Top Gear

1951
New cars introduced this year were Vauxhall's Wyvern and Velox, the French Simca and the new small Austin A30.

THE SCOTTISH MOTOR RACING CLUB

Although motor racing in Scotland started with the Sand Race Meeting at St Andrews in 1949 (at which the prizes were presented by Richard Attenborough), real circuit racing began with the Winfield Joint Committee (a co-operation between Berwick, Hawick and Lothian Car Clubs) meeting at Winfield airfield in 1950 where meetings continued until they moved their operations to the nearby Charterhall airfield in 1952.

In 1952 the Scottish Motor Racing Club was a joint organiser of a 500cc car race meeting at Kirkcaldy, and in 1956 the Border Motor Racing Club was formed. In 1964 these two Clubs merged, retaining the SMRC name.

Ian Scott-Watson was Secretary of the combined Club and re-opened negotiations, which had previously been unsuccessful, with the Royal Highland and Agricultural Society, with a view to creating a circuit at Ingliston utilising existing roads plus a new section. This circuit, which Ian Scott-Watson designed, was constructed during the winter of

The Ingliston Motor Racing Circuit
Photo courtesy Betty Craig

Andrew Morrison in a Mini-Cooper leads a trio at Knockhill
© W K Henderson

1964/65 for Scotcircuits Limited which had been formed, mainly by Office-Bearers of the SMRC with John Romanes as Chairman, to look after the commercial aspects of the venture. The SMRC conducted the racing with its pool of about 400 marshalling members, of which about 300 turned out for each of the six race meetings in the year.

This 3/4 mile mini-circuit was rather narrow but was much better than an airfield track. In 1968 it was extended to a mile in length which gave a much better straight section and a hairpin bend. Being well-placed between Edinburgh and Glasgow with all the facilities of the Royal Highland Showground, Ingliston was able to attract 12,000 at the opening meeting on 11 April 1965.

Race meetings were usually over-subscribed by competitors in many different classes, which encouraged drivers in Scotland and developed their talents for competition at other venues in Britain and, in some cases, internationally. It certainly fulfilled a long-felt desire in Scottish Motor Sport. Ingliston was always a user-friendly

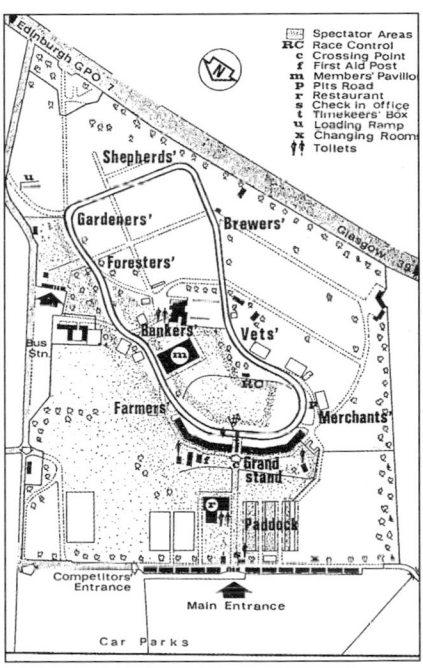

The layout at Ingliston

1952

Sydney Allard won the Monte Carlo Rally in a car of his own construction, still the only man to do so. But the simultaneous death of King George VI meant Allard barely got the publicity he deserved.

circuit and the team which ran the events changed very little over the years. Scottish motor racing owes a great deal to them.

After Derek Butcher took control of the circuit at Knockhill in Fife it was developed into an excellent 1.3 mile long circuit which can host a Scottish round of the exciting British Touring Car Championship.

Ingliston with its narrow and short track became inadequate for the faster cars and increasingly stringent safety regulations, so in 1995 the SMRC moved its racing events to Knockhill which was wider and longer.

N A Kennedy

The post-war ownership and increase in motor cars led to the growth of car clubs, each organising its own events. Reports of these activities were recorded in *Motor World,* a weekly publication covering all aspects of motoring and even boating, where Alistair Ford's couthy comments in "Pilot's World of Sport" column would bring a smile to the face of many competitors irrespective of their performance in the event concerned. The Scottish Sporting Car Club's journal, the original *Top Gear,* was a monthly publication and also contained reports of events and general articles on motoring.

Bigger rallies not only had class prizes but also offered a team award where the aggregate score of two or three competitors would be taken into account for the prize. Such teams entered under interesting names such as Ecurie Agricola (Border farmers) and Ecurie Courvoisier. The latter team was made up from members of the Lanarkshire Car Club during a 3-day event based in Braemar when they wanted a better title than the "Lanarkshire Car Club B Team". The name came in an inspiration in the bar one evening! This team even devised its own badge and went on to attract some 20 members. Although no longer competing they still meet for social gatherings remembering the "good old days".

Alan Carlaw

The JP - Scotland's racing car

While competing with a Cooper in 1949, Joe Potts from Bellshill pondered the idea of building a car of his own design. Construction began in the spring of 1950 with a view to running the car in the hill climbs of that year. The final design was eventually produced in two forms for the 1951 season when a light-weight model for Formula III racing and a Universal model for general use, and was powered by either 500, 1000 or 1100 cc J.A.P. engines. The car, without engine, painted to the customer's choice sold at £525 and provided stiff competition to the others in these classes.

THE NEW J.P. RACING CARS

'LIGHTWEIGHT' Model for FORMULA III.
'UNIVERSAL' Model for 500 c.c., 1,000 c.c. or 1,100 c.c. RACING

★ NEW Light Steel Tubular Chassis ★
★ PRECISION Rack and Pinion Steering ★
★ INDEPENDENT Suspension, Front & Rear ★
★ INDIVIDUAL Seating and Controls ★
★ LOCKHEED Hydraulic Brakes ★
★ £525 ex works, less engine ★

To all Motoring enthusiasts is extended an invitation to visit the Works at Bellshill, where the new J.P. Cars may be seen under construction.

JOSEPH POTTS LIMITED
NORTH ROAD, BELLSHILL, LANARKSHIRE

'EC' badge

The Triumphs of Ecurie Ecosse

It seems to have been David Murray's love of France which gave a Scottish motor-racing team the name of Ecurie Ecosse when it burst upon the scene in the early 1950s.

Murray had a chartered accountant's business in Edinburgh, with a few pubs to augment his income, but it was his dream of putting Scotland in the forefront of world motor racing that made him the public figure he was.

Murray (not to be confused with the later David Murray of Rangers Football Club) launched himself in racing in the late 1940s, won the Copenhagen Grand Prix and in 1951 took the courageous step of entering the World Championship Grand Prix Series as a private individual. When he raced in the British event at Silverstone, he was already in his forties.

Then Murray concentrated on managing his Ecurie Ecosse, gathering around him a group of fairly affluent amateurs, like Bill Dobson, Ian Stewart and Sir James Scott-Douglas.

From the modest base of their lock-up garages at Merchiston Mews in Edinburgh, Ecurie Ecosse became a name in world racing circles. Murray signed up a couple of dashing young Scots, Ron Flockhart and Ninian Sanderson, and on the team's very first attempt at the 24-hour classic of Le Mans in 1956 these two surprised everyone by taking first place.

The Esso Petroleum company, which had backed Ecurie Ecosse, gave a luncheon at the George Hotel in Edinburgh in September 1956 to celebrate what was undoubtedly a major victory.

David Murray was now much in favour with Jaguar, who offered him three factory D-types for the 1957 season. So he was set to return to Le Mans for what would be the 25th running of that famous classic. This time, however, the opposition would be stiffer.

For example, there would be the Ferrari team with Peter Collins/Phil Hill and Mike Hawthorn/Luigi Musso in the new

Ecurie Ecosse badge

'D' types being loaded into the transporter in Merchiston Mews under the supervision of Chief Engineer 'Wilkie' Wilkinson

Photo courtesy Wendy Jones

The Arrol-Johnston cars are making great headway among a class who look upon reliability as of primary importance. Already the large works at Underwood, Paisley are taxed to capacity. Mr Johnston, the manager, is making arrangements for an extension. Lord Roseberry is one of the latest users of an Arrol-Johnston.
Motor World - February 1902

1954
Coupons became a thing of the past as the Government declared the end of petrol rationing. Motorists were worried about the consequences of MoT testing by local garages.

4.1 litre Testa Rossas. Maserati had Stirling Moss and Harry Schell- while Aston Martin had Roy Salvadori and Les Leston.

This time David Murray teamed up Ron Flockhart with the Belgian Ivor Bueb, while his other entry had Ninian Sanderson partnered by John Lawrence, who had a garage business at Cullen in Banffshire.

Flockhart and Bueb gradually wore down the field and streaked home to win Le Mans for the second year running - followed in runner-up position by Sanderson and Lawrence!

For Ecurie Ecosse it was a colossal achievement by any standard. The success, however, may have blinded Murray to the fact that his cars were not powerful enough to compete with some of the emerging models.

Innes Ireland had been another famous name to join Ecurie Ecosse. But David Murray eventually departed the scene, leaving the supporters' club to enter Formula 2 racing in the 1970s. However it was an increasingly commercial world of motor sport and the original team sadly went out of business in 1971.

In 1983, Ecurie Ecosse was revived by Hugh McCaig, who had been a junior member in the earlier days and had become a well-to-do business man, running the circuit at Ingliston.

McCaig took the team back to international racing, back to Le Mans - and won the Group C2 World Sports Car Championship. But it was a very different sport from those early years and in 1989 Ecurie Ecosse entered into an association with Aston Martin.

The pioneering spirit of David Murray, however, had shown what can happen when you point your skills and enthusiasm towards an ideal - and set out to make a dream come true.

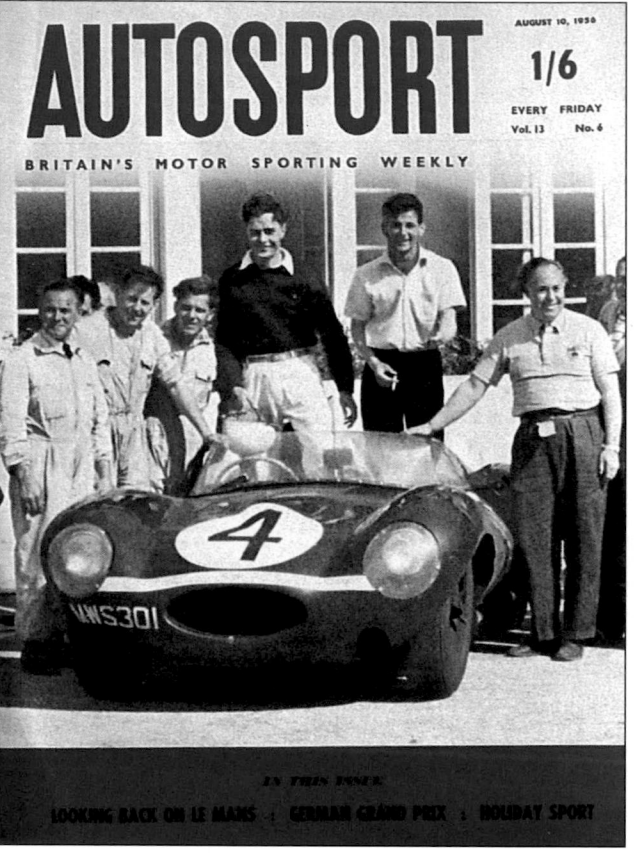

"VIVE L'ECURIE ECOSSE!"
Whilst David Murray, 'Wilkie' Wilkinson and the two mechanics stand happily beside the Le Mans-winning Jaguar, drivers Ron Flockhart and Ninian Sanderson register grins of triumph after their magnificent performance.
'Autosport's' customary red-printed cover was changed to blue for the edition of 10 August 1956 to highlight the victory.

*Le Mans 1957– this time first **and** second. Both 'D' type Jaguars are given the chequered flag.*
Photo courtesy of Stan Sproat

Le Mans 1957 – the team celebrate
Photo courtesy Wendy Jones

Scotland's Stars of Motor Sport

NINIAN SANDERSON

Ninian Sanderson, winner of the 24-hour classic at Le Mans in 1956, came of Border farming people before his father and uncle started Millburn Motors in Glasgow, where they built and operated coaches.

Ninian was born in May 1926, went to school at Strathallan and joined the Fleet Air Arm in the Second World War. A wild and mischievous spirit, Sanderson first tasted motor sport after the war when he was invited to the Highland Rally by Hartley Whyte, chairman of his family's Whyte and Mackay whisky company.

On the night before the rally Hartley and his wife Sheila taught Ninian and his wife Dorothy how to navigate on rallies. Ninian promptly went out next day - and won.

He went on to take fifth place in the Luxembourg Grand Prix of 1952 and David Murray invited him to join Ecurie Ecosse, the Scottish-based racing team. Ninian's father Bob bought him a C-type Jaguar for the purpose. So it was onward to his Ecurie Ecosse triumphs at Le Mans and beyond.

His business was in motor dealerships but that collapsed - and the man himself was overtaken by leukemia and cancer, from which he died in 1983. The actor Fulton Mackay gave the address at his farewell, a delightfully frank account of Ninian, and warned the heavenly authorities what to expect when the Ecurie Ecosse drove through the Pearly Gates!

Ninian Sanderson – often described as the rebel and buccaneer of the Scottish motor racing scene.
© Graham Gauld

ARCHIE SCOTT-BROWN

If ever there was a story of courage - and an inspiration for handicapped people everywhere - it must surely lie in the example of Archie Scott-Brown, who overcame the most severe disablement to take his proud place in the annals of motor racing.

The son of a flying ace from the First World War who then went into the motor trade in Paisley and Glasgow, Archie was born with a condition which was put down to the fact that his mother had German measles in 1927.

The subsequent ordeal was described by his biographer, Robert Edwards. An orthopaedic surgeon had to break his legs to straighten them and both feet had to be more or less amputated and re-attached the proper way round without destroying the nerves.

In a childhood of plaster-casts, callipers and surgical boots, he learned to walk after a fashion, leaning forward in a

Begrimed but smiling, Archie Scott-Brown in his Lister Jaguar after winning the sports car race in heavy rain at the European Grand Prix meeting, Aintree, Liverpool, July 1957
© The Herald

Archie Scott-Brown as caricatured by Sallon of the Daily Mirror in 1956
Courtesy Shell-Mex and BP Ltd

1955
The Le Mans race was won by Mike Hawthorns' D-type Jaguar. The Autocar reported – "Plainly, the D-type Jaguar is in production as a sporting road vehicle".
The last MG Midget, the TF, was replaced by the new MGA.

toppling position while swinging his arms to keep balance. By the age of eight it was clear his lower legs were not going to grow any more. And through all this his parents bought him a pedal car.

The maternal grandmother insisted that he wear an artificial hand to cover another of the disabilities but it "crippled and humiliated" him when he went to Merchiston Castle School, Edinburgh. The headmaster urged its removal.

When Archie went on to St Andrews University he found himself deeper in the contents of the *Autocar* than in his academic studies. Compensated with the looks of a film star, he developed into something of a personality – "a moustachio'd cavalier, quick with a joke, very handsome, a little on the short side, right arm inevitably shoved in the pocket of a nicely-cut tweed coat."

His mother separated from his alcoholic father and went to East Anglia with Archie when he became a sales representative for the Dobie tobacco company. When his grandmother left him £1000, however, he bought an MG TD car - and became part of the motor-racing scene of the 1950s.

Archie Scott-Brown drove the cars designed by Brian Lister, with engines developed by Don Moore. As he began to chalk up notable wins, people marvelled at the sheer guts of the man, able to use his left arm only for driving and with tiny legs which could hardly support his weight.

Constantly cheered on by his loving mother, Archie took the lead in the Belgian Sports Grand Prix at Spa-Francorchamps on 18 May 1958. Among the following cars was one driven by the young Jim Clark, who was forever haunted by what he saw next. Approaching a bend, Clark was faced with a pall of smoke as a Lister-Jaguar went off the wet track, somersaulted into the straw-bales and burst into flames. He knew it was his fellow-Scot, Archie Scott Brown, who died as a result of the severe burns.

In his biography, "Archie and the Listers," Robert Edwards told how hard it was to understand all those years later just how popular he was. Archie had enjoyed a relationship with the racing public and, more importantly, with his peers which

virtually no other British driver had ever approached.

Father and son used to sail around the Isle of Arran and it was to the Sleeping Warrior hill overlooking those waters of the Clyde that his father took Archie's ashes for scattering.

It was a sad end to the life which a very brave man had lived to its limits and beyond - an inspiring story which said so much for the sheer endurance of the human spirit.

INNES IRELAND

Flamboyant was the natural word to describe Innes Ireland, a dare-devil figure who blazed the trail by becoming the first Scotsman to win a Formula One Grand Prix.

The son of a veterinary surgeon from Kirkcudbright, Ireland had his moment of glory in the United States Grand Prix at Watkins Glen in 1961.

Born in 1930, Robert McGregor Innes Ireland became deeply interested in motor cars while still a boy, his attention arrested by a couple of Bentleys which were owned by a local lady of some wealth. In fact she bequeathed one of her models to the young enthusiast, who promptly drove it to his work as an apprentice mechanic!

During National Service with the King's Own Scottish Borderers and the Parachute Regiment he began to race his car in club events in 1954. As a keen patriot, Ireland was fiercely proud when given his first drive for Ecurie Ecosse, where he spent several seasons, sharing an ambition with its boss, David Murray, to advance the name of Scotland in the top echelons of world motor racing.

A friend of his family, Major Rupert Robinson, put money towards a Lotus Mark II sports car and Ireland was soon gaining attention as an up-and-coming driver.

Colin Chapman, who owned Lotus, was among those now aware of the flying Scotsman and gave him his first Grand Prix drive in 1959. Misfortune plagued Chapman's team,

Innes Ireland, winner of the American Grand Prix in 1961
© The Herald

It is rumoured that the Hon C S Rolls contemplates embarking in the automobile industry!
Motor World - May 1901

1956
Monaco's Prince Rainier married Irish-American film star Grace Kelly in April, making use of a Rolls-Royce Silver Wraith four-door convertible in their Monte Carlo wedding procession.
The Suez crisis brought about another fuel scare and petrol rationing to the British motorist.

however, and at the end of the season Ireland and the other works driver, Graham Hill, had to decide what they were going to do for 1960.

Hill moved on to BRM while Ireland, in a quandary but knowing that Chapman had a new car on the way, decided to stay with Lotus.

That was when the young Jim Clark joined the team, in time to see his fellow-Scot building up towards that American Grand Prix triumph of 1961.

It was a race in which Jack Brabham and Stirling Moss shot into the leading positions, with Innes Ireland suffering the added hazard that, in his troubled practise laps, he had disappeared into the trees and dented his fuel tank.

Though he eventually managed to take the lead he noticed that, with a reduced capacity, he was in danger of running out of petrol. Slowing down to save fuel, he was being pushed to the limit by Roy Salvadori. But he held on till the flag came down in his favour. Innes Ireland was the proudest man in the world. He had done it for Scotland.

Yet his finest moment was followed almost immediately by his worst. Within weeks he was stripped of his role as team leader at Lotus, replaced by his friend Jim Clark.

The latter denied that he had anything to do with the dismissal but it led to bad feeling and, much to Ireland's subsequent regret, there was not the chance to put it right. On Clark's death in 1968 he wrote a magazine article which was both a tribute and an apology.

So the colourful Innes Ireland never did win another Grand Prix, though he competed in 50 altogether. Having become president of the British Racing Drivers' Club, he retired in 1967 and sought a living in the motor trade among other things. He wrote for the Autocar magazine and was also motoring correspondent of the Sunday Standard, the Herald's weekend paper which ran through the early 1980s.

Innes Ireland had become a legend in his own lifetime, a popular figure who was full of exploits. He fought long against cancer but died in 1993 at the age of 63.

JIM CLARK

Scotland's first-ever world motor racing champion, Jim Clark, was always classed as a Borderer though he was actually born, in March 1936, at Kilmany in his mother's native kingdom of Fife.

His farming father was a Perthshire man and it was not until 1942, when Jim was six, that the Clarks moved south to the 1250 acres of Edington Mains at Chirnside, between Duns

Jim Clark
Painting by Senga Murray

and Berwick.

Who knows what stirs an interest in young minds? But, as a small boy, he rattled around in a little pedal car built by an uncle who was an enthusiast for cars.

From a well-heeled family he went to the fashionable Loretto School in Edinburgh, wielding a useful bat at cricket and showing signs of a good voice. But more and more he was reading motor racing magazines and by the age of sixteen – and not exactly an academic – he was back home on the farm, happy to be a shepherd and working on the land.

Jim Clark was the only boy, coming after four girls, and it was the husband of his oldest sister, Alex Calder, who was himself racing a Brooklands Riley 9, who took the lad to Ireland for the Ulster Trophy meeting at Dundrod.

The bug had bitten. He joined the Ednam Young Farmers' Club where he met Ian Scott Watson and Andrew Cowan, locals who were to become leading rally drivers. Indeed it seemed that people who joined the young farmers also joined Berwick and District Motor Club.

Young Clark started rallying with a Mark II Sunbeam Talbot and was showing such skill that Ian Scott Watson felt he was destined for motor racing, though his parents were already cutting back on pocket money to discourage such an idea.

There was no denying the inevitable however, and Jim Clark's racing career began, quite unexpectedly, in 1956 when he went north to act as mechanic to Ian Scott Watson at the wartime aerodrome of Crimond, between Peterhead and Fraserburgh, where the Aberdeen and District Motor Club had been holding meetings.

When Scott Watson came in from morning practice with his DKW Sonderclasse he said to Clark: "Go on, have a try. You're far enough away from home; your parents won't hear about it. Put on my helmet."

An excited Clark took the chance, put up a faster practise time than the owner, entered the race and, although he came last, had acquired a definite taste for motor racing. By chance, some of Jim's cousins were at Crimond that day and there were phone calls back to his Borders home with news of his adventure before his parents knew exactly where he was!

It was the unlikely start to a career in which he would spread his vast talent from touring cars and saloons to rallying, hill climbs and on to Formula One. In 1960 he joined Colin Chapman's Lotus team and soared to world championship level in a manner which had many people claiming him as the greatest racing driver of all time.

His record is certainly hard to beat. From only 72 Grand Prix starts, he produced a remarkable success rate of 25 wins, taking the world championship twice, coming third

Jim Clark looks at the rear of his Lotus – a view usually seen by other drivers!
Photo courtesy Betty Craig

1958

Although second to Moss at Casablanca, Mike Hawthorn beat him to the world championship by just one point after a thrilling season. However, Moss clinched the constructor's trophy for Vanwall, with Dutch, European, Moroccan, German, Italian and Portuguese GP wins.
The 948cc Austin-Healey Sprite was, at £678 on the road, the real sports car enthusiasts wanted. Its cheeky looks later earned it the 'Frogeye' tag.

Clark and Stewart sharing a joke at the 1965 British Grand Prix at Silverstone
© Eric Bryce

on two more occasions and, in 1965, becoming the first Briton to win the famous Indianapolis 500-mile race, setting a record average speed of 150.7 mph.

Drivers who went on to beat his actual number of Grand Prix wins included Jackie Stewart, Ayrton Senna, Alain Prost and Nigel Mansell but Clark's success rate remained the best.

The Borderer who sometimes looked more like a farmer than a racing driver was riding on the crest of his wave. Yet, as a sign of the changing times we now live in, you would find in the 1960s the Berwick and District Motor Club's dinner being graced by not only their local hero. Jim Clark would bring along with him racing legends including Graham Hill, Jack Brabham and Dan Gurney. At a later date, such rivals might hardly have been speaking to each other; but that was the spirit of the time.

Throughout his eight years at the top, Clark remained with Lotus. His mother said later that she felt he was going to retire in 1968 when he was 32. In the event, the decision was taken out of his hands.

On the Sunday afternoon of 7 April 1968 – I remember it with much the same shock as the Kennedy assassination – news reached us at the Daily Express office that Jim Clark was feared dead in a crash in Germany.

He had been competing in a fairly insignificant Formula Two race at Hockenheim when his Lotus skidded off the circuit and rammed into a tree. There was word of a blown-out tyre. Ironically, it was a part of Europe his father knew well, having been a prisoner of the Germans in the First World War.

The world mourned a quiet, unassuming man, good-looking but shy to the point of nail-biting and relaxed only with people he knew. He didn't smoke, drank little and lacked confidence with women, though he did have a lengthy relationship with a top model of the day, Sally Stokes.

After his death, his parents gave most of his racing trophies and awards to Duns Town Council and a Jim Clark Room was opened in the town in 1969. By the 1990s more than 200,000 people had visited this focal point of memory

and, to commemorate the 25th anniversary of his death in 1993, the room was refurbished and extended as a museum of his career, opened by his friend and rival, Jackie Stewart.

There was a very private and poignant moment in 1992 when that great racing driver, Ayrton Senna, flew into Edinburgh from Brazil to pay his own respects to the man who had been his inspiration.

After talking to pupils at Jim Clark's old school of Loretto (there is a plaque in his honour in the chapel) he drove on down to the Borders. And there, in a visit which went unrecorded at the time, Ayrton Senna stood in silent homage, little knowing that his own day was not far off, when he would go the Grand Prix of San Marino – and meet the same fate as his great hero, Jim Clark of Scotland.

COWAN to WALKINSHAW

Names flit across the pages of motoring history, often significant in the context of their own time but too easily forgotten in an age which sometimes neglects its heritage.

A 1990s Andrew Cowan beside his 1968 Hillman Hunter
© The Herald

The Berwickshire farmer Andrew Cowan, for example, was an important figure in rally driving within the opportunities of his day, before the modern marathons were invented.

Born in 1936, Cowan won the Scottish championship twice, driving a Sunbeam Rapier as part of the Rootes team. He won the Tour de France in 1964, the Alpine Rally of 1965, the Welsh Rally in 1966 and triumphed in his class at Monte Carlo before the decade was out.

As a member of the Mitsubishi Colt team he became a regular winner of the Southern Cross Rally in Australia and won the London-to-Sydney marathon of 1968, sharing the driving of the solo works Hillman Hunter with Colin Malkin. When the event was repeated in 1977 Cowan won again, this time as chief driver with Mercedes.

David Leslie, born in Dumfries in 1953, was in karting for 11 years, as a member of the British team, and won the European championship as well as clinching the Scottish title five times.

Leslie moved into Formula Ford 1600 racing in 1976 and was runner-up in the Stars of Tomorrow series. Into Formula Ford 2000, he was also runner-up in the British championships of 1978.

Leslie, who drove at Le Mans, made a major contribution to Scottish racing with his part in coaching the promising talent, young men like David Coulthard, Dario Franchitti and Allan McNish.

One remembers, too, glamorous names like Ron Flockhart, who started with motor cycles, later turning to sports cars and winning the Le Mans with Jaguar twice in the 1950s. Flockhart, born in 1924, was killed in a flying accident in 1962.

But few names in the sport have been more significant than that of Tom Walkinshaw. Born in the McRae country of Lanark, he was brought up at Prestonpans, where he rented a field on his father's farm and grew potatoes to sell from a van - the same van he used for transporting cars to compete at Ingliston and in the Scottish hill-climbs.

He won the Scottish Formula Ford championship in 1969, the British saloon car championship twice and the 1984 European Touring Car title. Tom Walkinshaw drove for Ecurie Ecosse, gained the Jim Clark Memorial Award and went on to mastermind the Jaguar victory at Le Mans in 1988, as well as three world sports-car titles.

The ambitious Scot bought a substantial stake in the famous Benetton team, where he became director of engineering - and persuaded the up-and-coming Michael Schumacher to join him. The German was soon world champion, hailed by some as the greatest Formula One driver of all.

But there was controversy surrounding Benetton cars and Walkinshaw moved over to the sister team of Ligier. His company worked on developing the Jaguar XJ220 as well as the Aston Martin DB7, before he teamed up with Volvo - and took his own Tom Walkinshaw Racing (TWR) into the British Touring Car Championships.

By then his group of 30 companies in the motor industry was employing 1000 people and showing a multi-million pound turnover. Walkinshaw had become a highly significant figure at the top end of world motor racing.

JACKIE STEWART

The motoring mood of Scotland perhaps had something to do with the fact that this small country managed to produce a second world motor-racing champion immediately on the heels of the first.

Jackie Stewart was three years younger than Jim Clark and, of the Grand Prix races in which they met, it was the established Clark who gained the upper hand, by 27 times to three.

But Stewart was just approaching his best years when Clark was killed in Germany in 1968 and, in the next five years, he went on to be world champion in 1969, 1971 and 1973, extending the Scottish dominance to an entire decade.

As so often in motor racing, there was rich romance in the

Tom Walkinshaw - head of the Oxfordshire based TWR Design who has now added the Arrows Formula One team to his £250m a year business empire.
© Autosport

1960
MoT tests and traffic wardens for London appeared for the first time and growing truck maker Leyland bought Standard-Triumph for £18 million. The growing popularity of cars on the road was partly behind the Beeching Report resulting in many rural branch railway lines being axed.

story of Jackie Stewart, from his early days in the family business of Dumbuck Garage at Milton, near Dumbarton.

His grandfather was a gamekeeper on the estate of the great Scottish industrialist Lord Weir and his father, Bob, used to fish regularly with his lordship. The story goes that, on the way to the fishing one day in 1926, Lord Weir pointed to a small roadside petrol station with its two hand-pumps and suggested that, with the rise of the motor car, that was surely a business for the future. He even offered to help in buying it but Bob Stewart raised the money himself.

Bob raced motor bikes in the Isle of Man TT races but now he had settled to making a living at Dumbuck. Jackie's brother Jimmy, who was eight years older, was first into motor-racing in 1953 so from an early age the youngster in this motor-mad family was taken to places like Silverstone, Goodwood and even Le Mans in 1954. As a star-struck

*"Back to school" - Jackie returns to Dumbarton Academy.
With him are Stirling Moss, son Paul
and lifelong friend John Lindsay.*
Photo courtesy of Nan Lindsay

schoolboy he dreamed of being a racing driver.

With a childhood sense of inadequacy - he was later found to be dyslexic - Jackie left school at 15 and set to work in his father's garage, priding himself in keeping the tidiest forecourt and being the best pump attendant.

It was there one day by chance that he caught first sight of his future friend and rival, Jim Clark, who was on his way to a hill-climb at Rest-and-be-Thankful. He had drawn in to fill up his TR2 when someone pointed him out as the bright young hope of the future, even if he hardly looked the part.

Despite his interest in cars, Stewart himself was diverted by football and a special talent for clay-pigeon shooting at international level, just missing out on an Olympic place in 1960.

So by modern standards he came late to the sport which would bring him fame, racing first at Charterhall in 1961, in a Marcos car which had a wooden chassis.

But by 1963 he was winning regularly with Ecurie Ecosse and soon he and Jim Clark were sharing a flat in London, often referred to as Batman and Robin. He credited Clark with showing him how to drive with finesse in Grand Prix racing.

Stewart entered his first Grand Prix in South Africa in 1965 and won later that year at Monza. He proceeded to be world champion three times, having beaten Clark's 25 GP wins, though from the greater opportunity of 99 starts.

Perhaps not so instinctive a driver as Clark, Stewart was nevertheless gifted with amazing reflexes. Despite approaches from Colin Chapman to join Clark, Stewart chose to stay with BRM, where he was the team-mate of Graham Hill.

He later joined Tyrrell, however, a move which was truly the making of his career. Clark's death was a devastating blow and, after three world championships, he pulled out of what would have been his 100th and last race following another tragedy, when team-mate Francois Cevert was decapitated.

But the shrewdness of Stewart had built many business contacts and the end of his racing days was just the start of

Jackie Stewart
© The Herald

another successful career. With Ford having provided the Tyrrell engines of his major triumphs, he extended his relationship as a consultant on the research and development of the company's products, having a hand in the engineering of cars like the Mondeo and Fiesta.

At the same time Jackie Stewart, who had moved to live in some splendour in Switzerland in 1968, backed one of his sons in a venture called Paul Stewart Racing. It built an impressive record in the lesser formulae, with drivers like David Coulthard in the stable.

In 1996 Jackie Stewart took that business dramatically to a new level by launching Stewart Grand Prix Racing, a return to the big-time through a five-year exclusive deal with Ford to supply him with V10 Cosworth-built engines. It was a deal worth £100 million.

So there were stirrings of a new era, with the old master at the business wheel, his son Paul gearing up as managing director - and a new vehicle of opportunity for young drivers to reach the very top of Formula One racing. Jackie Stewart did not build up false hopes. But there is not much in his impressive career which has been anything less than successful.

JOHN CLELAND

While Formula One racing gains more of the world limelight, aficionados tend to vote for the touring car scene when it comes to excitement. For a start, they can identify more closely with the vehicles, which bear a similarity to the ones they have at home; and the drivers are more accessible to the people who come to watch.

If there is a distance between the men who pilot the different disciplines, it is sometimes well expressed by Scotland's John Cleland, who runs a prosperous car dealership in Galashiels and won the British Touring Car Championship in 1995 for the second time.

In an age of image-builders and diplomatic quotes, the colourful Scot became a breath of fresh air as he cast aside

the mould of the mealy-mouth and gave us all the benefit of blunt opinion.

Cleland was the popular choice of the Association of Scottish Motoring Writers for their Jim Clark Memorial Award in 1996, a special joy for the Borderer who already took pride

Scottish stars of track and screen. Jackie with Sean Connery at Gleneagles Hotel
© The Herald

John Cleland - winner of the British Touring Car Championship in 1989 and 1995
© The Herald

in the fact that his BTCC trophy also bore the name of the Chirnside hero.

In the days when Grand Prix drivers would turn up at other levels too, Jim Clark carried off the touring trophy in 1964, just 25 years before Cleland gained his first victory.

The man from Gala, who sold Volvos while racing Vauxhalls, had his first taste of motor-sport as an apprentice with Triumph at Coventry, when he appeared in a Herald for a Midlands driving test. Cleland could then be found driving a Mini in the hill climb at Kinkell, near St Andrews in 1971, a Chevron at Ingliston and a Colt Lancer in the 1976 Scottish rally championship, where he was hailed as best newcomer.

In the 1980s he found his true role in production saloons, from an Opel Ascona to the Vauxhall Carlton. When he won the British Touring Car Championship for the first time in 1989 he was in a Vauxhall Astra.

But the Cavalier was on its way and in his sixth year of driving and developing it, he carried off his second BTCC win at the age of 43.

John Cleland has been known to bemoan the lack of characters, people with humour, at what is often seen as dreary Grand Prix press conferences. He himself became the best guarantee that there could be no such criticism in the touring class!

THE McRAE FAMILY

Heading towards the top of his chosen sport, Colin McRae from Lanark made some pointed comments about what he regarded as a lack of media attention given to rallying.

Appropriately, it was McRae himself who remedied the matter in 1995 when he became Britain's first world rally champion and the youngest man ever to capture that crown.

It was a remarkable feat, breaking into a scene which had been dominated by continental drivers all the way from Finland to Italy; and it was clinched in Britain's own RAC Rally which had been more usually a platform for those overseas stars, much in the way that Wimbledon has been for

tennis.

But the gritty young Scot changed all that and, in doing so, added the finest chapter to the story of the incredible McRaes, which must be without parallel in motor-sport.

Though father Jimmy, a typically down-to-earth Scot, came rather late on the scene for gaining a world place, he nevertheless carried off the British rally championship no fewer than five times between 1982 and 1988.

By then the eldest of his three sons, Colin, was snapping at his heels and re-capturing that title for the Lanark family within a few years of his father. By the time he had retained the title and gone on to prepare for even greater things, it was the turn of second son Alister to come through and make it eight British championships for this astonishing family.

Capping it all, of course, was the 1995 triumph of Colin who certainly gave rallying in this country the publicity boost he felt it needed. Not that it was so lacking in attention from

The McRaes – father Jimmy flanked by sons Colin and Alister
© Evening Times

Colin McRae and Glasgow based navigator Derek Ringer after their victory in New Zealand for the Subaru World Rally Team
© Evening Times

During the past year more cars per thousand of population were sold in Scotland than in any other country in the world except the USA. That may seem a tall statement but it is nevertheless almost certainly true.
Motor World - November 1910

1963
In London, Lesney made its 35 millionth Matchbox toy car. Mystery ginger hairs found clogging carburettor jets in new Minis were traced to orange dusters being used to prepare metal fuel tanks.

the general public.

As McRae and his fellow-drivers covered those 1445 miles of England, Wales and the Scottish Border, ending up in Chester, they were watched by well over two million spectators, with extensive coverage on television throughout the world.

It was the eighth and final round of the championship and the Scot's victory was all the more commendable in view of what happened in the previous month's Catalonian rally.

McRae's more experienced team-mate in the British-based Prodrive-Subaru team was the famous Carlos Sainz of Spain, twice world champion and regarded as perhaps the finest all-round driver of all. McRae was evidently ordered to let Sainz pass him and win the Catalonian "for commercial reasons," leaving both drivers to approach the RAC Rally on level points to secure the manufacturers' prize.

McRae was less than enamoured of the situation and said as long as he lived he would never understand it. When it came to the crunch however it was each man for himself and Colin McRae, despite the handicap of a burst tyre, proved that, at the age of 27, he was the best rally driver in the world.

He also gave due credit to the man by his side, Glasgow-based Derek Ringer, who won the world title for co-drivers. Ringer had gained an interest in motor sport as a student in the 1970s and became an engineer with Ferranti. He had no intention of driving for a career until he struck up his partnership with the man from Lanark.

Colin McRae had the advantage of his father's example and his potential was also recognised by the Subaru team boss, David Richards, when he came sixth in the 1990 RAC Rally in a battered Ford Sierra. Richards became a key influence and his faith was finally rewarded.

The growing stature of McRae meant a corresponding change in his lifestyle. With a reported salary of more than £250,000, he had homes in the convenient tax-haven of Monte Carlo and in the Swiss Alpine resort of Verier.

Though he had also expressed an interest in Formula One, his proven forte had been rally-driving, consolidating that family achievement which gave the McRaes of Lanark their quite unique place in motor-sport history.

DAVID COULTHARD

Since the heady days of Jim Clark and Jackie Stewart, Scotland may not have produced another world champion but it has not been without its representatives on the tracks of Grand Prix racing.

David Coulthard
© The Herald

Jim Crawford from Dunfermline and Johnny Dumfries (the Marquis of Bute) kept their country in touch with the top end of the sport in the 1980s, the courageous Crawford going on to Indy racing and surviving the surgery from a horrendous crash to race again with considerable handicap. But if he and Dumfries did not bring home the top accolades it was an indication of how slender is the line between success and failure.

Towards the 1990s,

however, came the younger crop of Scottish hopefuls, including Allan McNish from Dumfries and Dario Franchitti from Whitburn. But the one who broke through the barrier to Grand Prix success - the first since Jackie Stewart in 1973 - was David Coulthard, the haulage contractor's son from the Kirkcudbright village of Twynholm who reached the top step

of the podium when he won the Portuguese prize at Estoril in September 1995 (Estoril had a lucky ring for the Scots, as the base of Jock Stein's famous Lisbon Lions when Celtic won the European Cup in 1967).

It raised hopes of even greater things for the lad, born on 27 March 1971, whose instinct took him to karting as a child

Words of wisdom from Jackie Stewart before the 1996 Australian Grand Prix at the Albert Park circuit in Melbourne
© The Herald

1965
The new 70mph speed restriction was tried for four weeks, and became permanent from 22 December, a few days before Barbara Castle became the first woman transport minister.

and who was already dominating that sport by the age of 12, when he became the country's junior champion.

By 18 he had broken through to single-seater racing, winning the Junior Formula Ford championship. He then came under the influence of Jackie Stewart when he joined Paul Stewart Racing, run by the former world champion's son as a structural staircase to the top for those with the talent to climb it.

There he was driving a £250,000 180mph Formula 3000 machine and Jackie Stewart was among those in no doubt that Coulthard had the potential to go all the way.

He gathered awards which ranged from the most promising driver to race at Silverstone to the McLaren/Autosport Young Driver of the Year, with its opportunity to test-drive a McLaren Honda.

In 1993 he drove for Jaguar in the Le Mans 24-hour race and was a member of the team which won the GT class. By 1994 he had started as a test driver for the Williams team and was due to compete in a F3000 race at Silverstone. Before the race that day he received a hand-written fax-message from Ayrton Senna the Williams team leader, wishing him all the best. It was on that very day that the great Brazilian was killed in the San Marino Grand Prix. Coulthard was shattered.

Damon Hill became the Williams team leader and young Coulthard was promoted from test driver. In his debut season he ended in eighth place but there followed a controversy when he was sidelined in favour of Nigel Mansell, who was brought back from his adventures in America. There was also a contractual dispute with Williams and Coulthard joined McLaren Mercedes in time for the 1996 season.

But the young Scot was already being hailed as having skills and confidence well beyond his years. He gave notice of his place among the fastest drivers by out-qualifying the world champion, Michael Schumacher, to take pole position for three successive Grand Prix, at Monza, Estoril and Nurburgring.

There was a feeling he would do it in 1995 and the Portuguese victory confirmed that faith. David Coulthard was also blessed with a tower of strength at his back - the dedication of his haulage contractor father Duncan, a frustrated racing driver if ever there was one, who might have been a formidable competitor if there had not been a family business to run.

David triumphant at the 1995 Portuguese Grand Prix
© The Herald

LOUISE AITKEN-WALKER

Louise Aitken-Walker from Duns in Berwickshire carved her own piece of motor-sport history in 1990 when she became Scotland's first world rallying champion.

She gained the women's title five years before fellow-Scot Colin McRae from Lanark followed through with the men's championship, giving their native land a famous double.

Louise, romantically described as a Borders shepherdess, left the family fields to test herself in the 1979 contest in which Ford wanted to find a woman rally driver. She won it.

A decade later she was heading for the world Championship at the wheel of a Vauxhall Astra. Not that Louise's championship year was without its drama. In fact she and her Swedish co-driver, Tina Thorner, figured in a spectacular plunge into a Portuguese lake, forcing them to smash their way out of the upturned car before swimming for their lives.

In 1983, the young Scot became the first woman to win a British national championship outright, in an RS2000 Escort. And when the world-beating Vauxhall team was disbanded she drove for Ford in selected British championship events.

Louise Aitken-Walker was honoured with the MBE in 1992 and has also been the recipient of two awards in memory of the late Jim Clark, twice the world Grand Prix champion, who also came from Duns.

In Louise's brave attempt to maintain a remarkable reputation for such a small area, there was always the sense of regret that she didn't have the top-grade equipment to support her talents.

But she gained her fame nevertheless, before standing down from racing to have her family.

Louise, after receiving her MBE at Buckingham Palace in May 1992
© The Herald

Sasha Pearl

Farm girl Sasha Pearl from Perthshire, was the top lady finisher in the 1995 Elf Renault Clio UK cup. The Flying Scot won the championship despite fierce opposition, no mean feat as the Coupe des Dames is aimed at female drivers contesting this series which is part of the now very popular British Touring Car Championships.

1967
The death occurred this year of speed king Donald Campbell who died on Coniston Water trying to break the world water speed record.

Louise Aitken-Walker regarded as Britain's foremost lady rally driver
© The Herald

The Motor Trade

In a land which showed such an early interest in building the motor car, it is appropriate that the Scottish Motor Show, which attracts large crowds to Glasgow every two years, should rank with Paris as the oldest event of its kind in the world. It also has the distinction of being the only one run by the motor trade and not the manufacturers.

It is true that the first gathering of cars on display had to take its modest place at what was then the Edinburgh Cycle Show of 1897. But the fact that Scottish engineers were by then turning serious attention to this new form of transport was soon reflected in the models on show.

By 1903, the Waverley Market event had become the Edinburgh Motor and Cycle Show and the growing influence of the new-found trade was seen that same year in the formation of the Scottish Motor Manufacturers and Traders' Association. For its first president, that gathering of car makers, coachbuilders and retail people chose John Stirling of Hamilton, whose car showroom in Sauchiehall Street was the very first in Glasgow.

Other prominent people of the day who were involved included Harry Prosser and Andrew Rennie, names which survived to modern times; and AC Penman of Dumfries whose company built bodies for Albion and Arrol-Johnston.

The association, which trimmed its title to the Scottish Motor Trade Association (SMTA), we know today, bought out the cycle dealers and took over the full running of the exhibition from 1908, by which time the motor car was well established in Scotland.

Progress could be gauged from figures given at the third annual supper of the association in 1906. Whereas there had been 3000 cars registered in Scotland by 1904, the number had risen to 5000 two years later.

Waverley Market in Edinburgh was not the most comfortable of venues, however, and in 1920 the show was

The COAT OF ARMS of the Scottish Motor Trade Association

An early photograph, probably taken in 1904, at the Waverley Market, venue of the first Scottish Motor shows
Photograph courtesy SMTA

Austin, Humber and Armstrong-Siddeley cars displayed at the Kelvin Hall Motor Show in the 1920s.
Photograph courtesy SMTA

1968
The first scheduled Hovercraft service between Dover and Boulogne was inaugurated on 1 August. The SRN4 "Mountbatten" carried 30 cars and 250 passengers. British Motor Holdings and Leyland merged to form British Leyland. The new company made a staggering 46 different types of car.

John D Brimlow then of the Stirling Motor Company and later Argylls Ltd convened the inaugural meeting of the SMTA in April 1903.
Photograph courtesy SMTA

John Stirling, the SMTA's first president. It was from Stirling's Madelvic factory at Granton that the first buses to run in Australia came from
Photograph courtesy SMTA

moved to the old Kelvin Hall in Glasgow.

In those days, well-known Scottish names like Argyll and Arrol-Johnston were taking their place alongside Rolls-Royce, Lanchester and Wolseley and American cars like the Buick, which was founded by a Scot, David Buick from Arbroath.

Ventilation in that first Kelvin Hall, however, was so bad that motor people shed no tears when it was burned down. The show went back to Edinburgh for 1925 but returned to Glasgow with the building of a splendid new Kelvin Hall, the one we know today.

And there the Motor Show remained until the 1980s, when they built the spacious Scottish Exhibition and Conference Centre, coincidentally on the banks of the Clyde at Finnieston Street, which already had an affinity with motor cars. For it

*"VARIOUS BRANDS OF SCOTCH!"
as sampled by cartoonist Frank Leah
at the 1922 Scottish Motor Show in Glasgow*
Photograph courtesy SMTA

was on that very street, at the beginning of the century, that Albion Motors made their first cars, both Halley and Carlaw their commercial vehicles and Walter Bergius turned out his Kelvin car.

In fact the Scottish Motor Show became the curtain-raiser for the new SECC when it opened its doors in 1985. Two years later it attracted a record crowd of 170,000. The show, which had gone on to a two-yearly basis, is still run by a subsidiary of the SMTA.

That association still flourishes after 100 years of the motor car in Scotland, serving 1100 members as a powerful voice for the industry.

It is fitting that the Kelvin Hall, still remembered fondly as the venue of the Motor Show, should now house the splendid Glasgow Museum of Transport, displaying all that was best from those early days of the motor car, when Scotland awakened to the excitement of a transport revolution.

The commercial vehicle section of a Kelvin Hall show with trucks, vans and buses in evidence

Photo courtesy SMTA

The car section of the cramped confines of a Kelvin Hall Motor Show

Photo courtey SMTA

The more spacious halls of the Scottish Exhibition & Conference Centre at Finnieston, Glasgow is now the venue for the Scottish Motor Show seen here in 1995

Photo courtesy SMTA

"Glasgow's new highway" gives details for proposed town planning in the Glasgow Corporation Scheme which embraces lands in the districts of Kelvinside, Temple, Jordanhill, Broomhill, Whiteinch, Scotstoun, Yoker East, Drumchapel, Scotstounhill and Knightswood and includes in its main features the construction of a wide thoroughfare from Anniesland to Clydebank borough boundary. It was stated that the whole of the area was likely to be developed in the near future and it was estimated there would be a population of around 180,000 embraced in the scheme. In a reference to the proposed boulevard from Anniesland it was said that Dunbartonshire had agreed to co-operate with Glasgow in the extension of the road.
Motor World - 5 February 1915

1970
Jack Brabham, grand prix's longest serving driver, announced his retirement shortly after three fatalities in the sport – Bruce McLaren, Piers Courage and the 1970 world champion Jochen Rindt, whose title was awarded posthumously.

Office Bearers 1994–1996
George Watt James Hird
SMTA President SMTA Vice-president

Looking after the interests of both the consumer and the respectable motor trade is the dual aim of the Scottish Motor Trade Association. Its 1,250 members range from small non- franchised service and repair outlets to large multi-franchise motor retailing groups which are household names. Each member of the Association, however, agrees and undertakes to abide by the Code of Practice for the Motor Industry, endorsed by the Office of Fair Trading, and the SMTA Code of Conduct and also conforms to strict standards of both premises and service. The Association also offers a custom made mechanical breakdown insurance policy to its members customers.

ARNOLD CLARK

Every part of the country has its own story of a local car dealer who has built up a successful business and become a household name in the process.

Those stories are perhaps symbolised by that of Arnold Clark, who became Scotland's biggest car retailer during the second half of the century.

In an area sometimes tainted by the image of the shady dealer, Arnold Clark emerges as the kirk elder and staunch family man, surrounded by long-service employees who have stayed as loyal to him as the customers who have kept coming back.

"I used to be ashamed to tell people I was a car dealer because they looked at you as if you were a crook," he once said. "So I made up my mind that I would never give anyone any reason to call me that. I have tried to run an honest business."

In doing so, he took his group into the mid-1990s with a turn-over of more than £300 million, with sales of 40,000 new and used cars per year, and employing more than 1700 people at 37 showrooms and 44 garages. By that time he had no fewer than 17 different manufacturing franchises.

Arnold Clark's ability to deal with big numbers was also reflected in his own life, where he had nine children from two marriages, with a family commune which even had room for two mothers-in-law.

He has never failed to credit the basis of his success to the good standards which prevailed in the working-class environment of the old Glasgow tile-close. It was there that he learned about hard work and fair play - and how to live in harmony when you were a mixture of Catholics, Protestants and Jews.

The son of a steelworker at the Blochairn Works, Arnold Clark joined the RAF at the end of the Second World War, was trained as a mechanic and began to buy and sell cars when he returned to civilian life.

By 1954 he had accumulated enough capital to open his

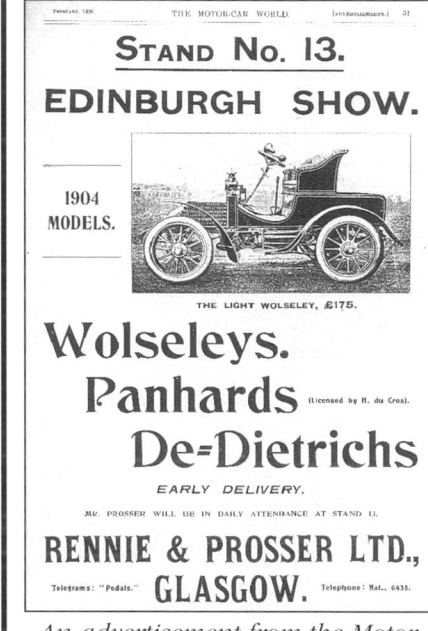

An advertisement from the Motor-Car World of February 1904

Glasgow Exhibition trials run over five days. Of the 53 vehicles entered 45 started. Runs of about 100 miles each day were made to Edinburgh, Ayr, Callander, Stirling and Glen Devon and to Tyndrum.
Motor World - September 1901

1971
W O Bentley died and Rolls-Royce, the company making his cars, spectacularly went bust depite its new Corniche with a hefty power boost.

first showroom, in Park Road, Glasgow, a sentimental connection which he did not sever. Waiting until he had enough capital to finance his ambitions became part of the business philosophy of Arnold Clark. He had never forgotten his father's warnings about debt.

It was only in later years, when the business exploded out of all recognition, that he entered into any kind of overdraft. Stage by stage the expansion came: Bothwell Street, Eglinton Street, Paisley, Bearsden, Bishopbriggs, Kilmarnock, Elderslie.

In 1959 he gained his first franchise from Morris. Then came Jaguar, Rootes, Triumph, Rover and onwards to Vauxhall, Audi/Volkswagen and Renault.

Arnold Clark – Chairman & Joint Managing Director

The Arnold Clark Citroen outlet at the Phoenix Retail Park in Linwood opened in 1995

As it reached the sixth place in the UK motoring world for pre-tax profitability, it was still an all-family business. Contract hire became a large part of the business during the 1980s, though Arnold Clark had been experienced in that sphere since the 1960s.

Much of the firm's expansion has come from acquisition, dating from West End Motors, which gave him Rootes and Jaguar. All have been absorbed into the company image, except the famous old name of Macharg, Rennie and Lindsay, which had the distinction of being allowed to trade with its own identity. Arnold Clark had had a good personal relationship with Mr Macharg over many years.

So the company extended to Edinburgh and Aberdeen and most other corners of Scotland. Appropriately for a major car dealer, Arnold Clark opened in Phoenix Park at Linwood, right on the site of the former Rootes (later Chrysler) enterprise which gave Scotland its only experience of the mass production of cars, during the 1960s.

Like many a self-made businessman, Arnold Clark needed another dimension to his life and found it in art, becoming something of a connoisseur and enthusiastic collector of paintings.

MORRISONS GARAGE

In 1925 Mr Archie Morrison opened a cycle and motor cycle repair shop in Stirling and two years later moved to a green-field site at Whins of Milton. He told the story that the removal was done by Wordie Brothers, a local firm of carters, and he gave the driver of the horse and cart a tip of two shillings. The driver looked at the tip and then looked at Mr Morrison and said "I think, laddie, you're in more need of this than me". Little did the driver know that the business would grow from that small wooden hut into the modern complex now standing. The firm now hold the Rover, MG and Land Rover & Range Rover franchises with the third generation family now involved in the business. Sandy Morrison was president of the SMTA in 1974/75 and he and his brother Logan participated in motor sport in the 1950s and 60s both being past Scottish Rally Champions. Logan's son Andrew now drives a Mini-Cooper at Knockhill and Doune.

Morrison's Garage in the 1930s.
Cars seen include a Standard, Riley, Humber, Morris,
MG and motor cycle combination.
Petrol pumps selling Redline, National Benzole and Shell.

GLASGOW'S CARRIAGEWAY OF CARS

The congregation of motor trade outlets in the same area is nothing new. By the early 1930's Glasgow's Bothwell Street was a motorists' mecca and a glance at the 1939 Glasgow Post Office Directory reveals a number of firms and franchises long since forgotten. Running down the list you see Robert Gibson & Sons Motors Ltd at number 11, A & D Fraser Ltd (Morris and MG) at 39 - 49, David Carlaw & Sons Ltd (Austin) at 81 , Taggarts (Glasgow) Ltd, 85 - 87, Armour and Melvin Ltd at 91, H Prosser & Sons (Wolseley) at 123, M MacIntyre Ltd at 133 , Prosser again at 139 , George & Jobling (Allard) at 140 - 160, Scott Brown & Company 147 - 155, and Cameron & Campbell Ltd 171 - 181. Motor trade associated businesses included James H Lightbody (motor trade supplier), the Scottish Motor of Trade Association, The Scottish Motor & Cycle Manufacturers and Factors Association, the Motor Taxation Department and fuel, tyre and equipment manufacturers. By 1951 Carlaws were no longer in Bothwell Street, Rossleigh was at 147 and S Smith & Sons, the instrument suppliers, were at 151-153 but the Street remained virtually unchanged until the development of the Albany Hotel and Heron House in the 1970s. Although many of these firms no longer exist some have been bought over and others have emerged in their place. The motor trade in Scotland has adapted to the changes in the marketplace and faces the next century with confidence.

The showroom of H Prosser & Sons,
123 - 127 Bothwell Street in 1934
© Glasgow City Archives

1973
Britain, gripped by the Arab oil embargo and miners' strikes – heralding rocketing fuel prices and the three-day week respectively – saw petrol coupons issued and a voluntary 50mph speed limit.

The Royal Scottish Automobile Club

Above the bustle of central Glasgow, Blythswood Square stands high and dignified – an appropriate setting for the Royal Scottish Automobile Club, which occupies the whole of its eastern side.

It is the nerve-centre of Scotland's senior motoring organisation, not only providing the comfort and convenience of a fully-fledged club, where members can dine, wine, entertain or spend the night, but earning a reputation for its leadership in motor sport and its watchdog role in matters of legislation affecting every car-owner.

Among the features of the clubhouse, displayed at the top of the central staircase you can gaze upon such motoring memorabilia as the helmets of Scottish racing legends Jim Clark and Jackie Stewart.

Indeed Stewart figures prominently in the membership to-day, along with other familiar names like Andrew Cowan and the McRae family, who have taken Scotland into the top bracket of international rally driving.

The origins of the RSAC date back to those early days of motoring, at the tail-end of the 19th century. Whereas in London they formed the Royal Automobile Club in 1897, the Scottish counterpart came into existence with just days to spare before the bells rang in the New Year of 1900.

At that time it was known as the Scottish Automobile Club,

One of the Club's first car badges
© Alan Carlaw

founded in Edinburgh with an eastern and western section. It soon became evident, however, that the emphasis of Scotland's motor industry would lie in the industrial west, prompting the decision to establish clubhouse premises in Glasgow.

The first president was the Rt Hon Sir John Macdonald, Lord Chief Justice Clerk of Scotland (he became Lord Kingsburgh), and it was under his guidance that, in 1909, the pioneers of the club bought the terraced house at No.11 Blythswood Square for £4,500.

As the neighbouring houses became available, they bought them up, left and right, till James Miller, the distinguished architect, could be engaged to remodel that whole side of the square as one entity, creating a central hall and dining-room, much as we see them today, with that impressive staircase leading to the lounge and function rooms of the first floor.

During the First World War the club took on the

The Club's imposing Blythswood Square building
© Chris Christodoulou

A meeting of gentlemen interested in automobilism was held in the Royal Hotel, Edinburgh to consider a proposal to form a Scottish Automobile Club associated with the Automobile Club of Great Britain and Ireland. There was an attendance of about twenty presided over by Mr John McDonald. Mr C Johnstone, the secretary of the Automobile Club explained the purposes for which the body had been formed and the uses it would serve in the way of developing automobilism throughout the country and of obtaining uniform traffic regulations. On the motion of Dr Turner, seconded by Mr John Wilson, it was agreed to form a club in Scotland affiliated to the Automobile Club of Great Britain and Ireland. The Lord Justice Clerk, in supporting the movement, said he looked upon automobilism as a new and very pleasant branch of sport.
Motor World - December 1899

1974
New cars included the wedge-shaped Lotus Elite, the VW Golf, Citroen CX and Porsche 911. VAT was imposed on petrol and a bankrupt British Leyland was forced to go cap-in-hand to the government.

An early rally of SAC members to Philiphaugh in May 1901. The start was from Charlotte Square, Edinburgh in procession but once outside the City each car made its own pace.
Photo courtesy RSAC

unexpected role of providing cars to transport the wounded as they arrived home from the front. And that was how King George V came to grant the "Royal" prefix in 1917.

Beyond the social convenience of its own premises in central Glasgow, the Royal Scottish Automobile Club keeps a constant eye on the law as it affects the motorist. In this respect it shares a standing joint committee with the AA and RAC.

But not least of its achievements is to be found in motor sport, where the hill climbs and reliability trials of an earlier day have been succeeded by the International Scottish Rally, which was run for the fiftieth time in 1995.

Like the RAC Rally down south, the Scottish one began in 1932 and would have been first to reach the half-century mark if a tanker-drivers' strike at Grangemouth in 1974 had not scuppered the event through shortage of fuel.

Those early hill climbs and trials could make or break the models of the day but, as the cars themselves became more

Robert John Smith – first secretary of the Club
Courtesy RSAC

reliable, the importance of these events began to wane.

So the rally took over in 1932 – and not without an emphasis on the social side. As Jonathan Lord, secretary of the RSAC, has pointed out, the dinner jacket was de rigueur for the evening festivities and the best hotels were used for overnight stops. After all, competitors had been promised "a

*The Earl of Elgin, President of the Club, chats to past secretary
A K Stevenson and his successor R Tennant Reid*

Photo courtesy RSAC

*Watched by a large crowd, Lord Provost Myer Galpern
flags off a Jowett Javelin at the Glasgow start of the
1952 Monte Carlo Rally from Blythswood Square*

© Photo courtesy RSAC

*Despite the weather, enthusiasts examine the cars
for the Glasgow start of the 1958 Monte Carlo Rally*

© Alan Carlaw

The Club Badge
© Alan Carlaw

pleasant, sporting and romantic tour" of some of Scotland's
most scenic areas.

Among the cars taking part in that first Scottish Rally was a
Napier, now the property of the RSAC's president, the Earl of
Elgin and Kincardine. Always a keen supporter of the event,
Lord Elgin once took part in a Rolls-Royce, though that was
before they brought in the forest stages!

Even in pre-war days, there was never any shortage of
self-generated publicity. You would find that the participants
included celebrities like Amy Johnson, the great female flyer
of her day, who happened to be married to that other famous
pioneer of flight, Jim Mollison, a native of Glasgow.

In 1938, the spectacular Empire Exhibition at Bellahouston
Park, Glasgow, became a focal point of the rally, as did the
Garden Festival of 50 years later, when Jimmy McRae secured
his victory.

The club's annual Veteran, Vintage and Classic Car Run
offers a less hectic form of motor sport.

*"Practical points" - Do not use a
big spanner on a small nut.
You are only risking the
shearing of the thread. There is
nothing in which the amateur is
more apparent than in the
simple operation of tightening a
nut.*
Motor World - 9 April 1908

1976
*The previously codenamed
"Bobcat" small Ford emerged as
the new neat Fiesta hatchback,
built in Spain.*

"Round the bend" – starter from Glasgow, Andrew McCracken with Jimmy and Arlene McInnes in their Ford Anglia in the Alps during the 1961 Monte Carlo Rally
Photo courtesy Arlene McInnes

Le Rallye Automobile Monte-Carlo 1961 programme cover
Courtesy Arlene McInnes

A well-thumbed cover of the 1961 Rally regulations
Courtesy Arlene McInnes

Back in the club at Blythswood Square, members enjoy their meal in a splendid ambience, repairing either to the Rally Bar or to another with a motoring connotation, the Argyll, recalling that famous pioneering name of Scottish motor manufacture.

There is a sense of history and permanence symbolised by men like R J Smith, who held the post of secretary from 1899 till his death in 1942. It was through Smith's initiative that road-signs were erected in towns and villages throughout Scotland, some of them surviving to this day.

As a tribute to his work, the members presented him with a Daimler bearing the coveted registration number G1, the very first number issued in Glasgow. Mr Smith was succeeded by A K Stevenson, who was long associated with the British start of the Monte Carlo Rally.

In 1926 that start took place from John O' Groats but by 1952 it had moved to Blythswood Square, Glasgow, where large crowds gathered to watch the Lord Provost flag away the drivers on the long journey to the Mediterranean.

So there is a broad base to the activities of the Royal Scottish Automobile Club, whose members also enjoy a reciprocal arrangement with 170 other clubs around the world.

The Rest and be Thankful, an elevation of 860 feet, has been immortalised by the poet Wordsworth –
"Doubling and doubling with laborious walk,
Who, that has gained at length the wished-for height;
Tis brief, this simple wayside call Can slight and rests not to be thankful."
Motor World - July 1910

Since the motorist became such a recognised part of the community no event has stirred them so deeply as the news of the death of Sir John MacDonald. He was the head of the motor car movement in Scotland and a personality of influence in a wider sphere. The late President of the RSAC was a man of many parts, and it would be wrong to say that his chief interest lay in motoring, though applied to his later years that statement is true.
Motor World - May 1919

1977
In the year that Elvis Presley, the King of rock 'n roll died of a heart attack, car business rumours abounded. Would Donald Healey buy Reliant? Would the De Lorean be built in Puerto Rico? Would Volvo merge with Saab?

Nigel Kennedy's Burdmonk rounding the Hairpin bend at the RSAC's Rest and be Thankful Speed Hill Climb.

Photo courtesy Nigel Kennedy

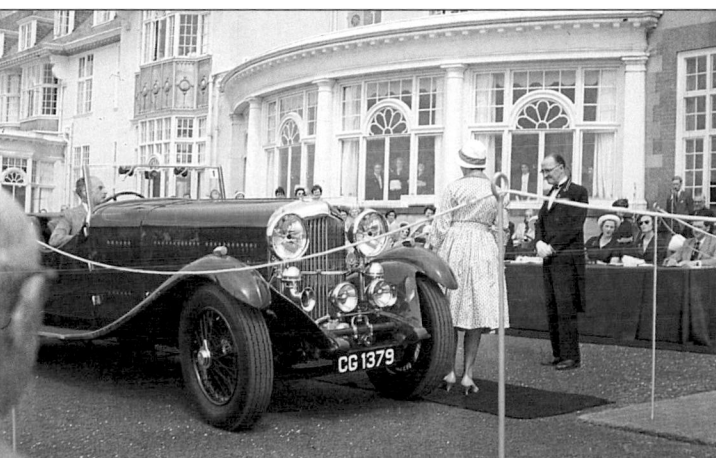

Concours d'Elegance – Hartley Whyte's 8-litre Bentley tourer at Turnberry Hotel in the early 1960s.

Photo courtesy Stuart Parker

Programme for the 1951 Rest and be Thankful Speed Hill Climb

Basil Davenport, one of Britain's best known hill climb competitors, in his home-built G N Spider Special car on the Rest and be Thankful.

Photo courtesy RSAC

1951 Scottish Rally programme

1978

Chrysler sold its entire European operations to Peugeot, thus creating Europe's biggest car company in France. De Lorean announced plans to make his car in Northern Ireland with £52 million of British government backing.

Line up of cars on the 1959 RSAC Veteran Run
© Alan Carlaw

1996 Scottish Rally Regulations.
The first RSAC Scottish Rally was held in 1932, and the event was held annually until the outbreak of war in 1939. Revived in 1951, and with the exception of the years 1957, 1960 and 1974, it has been run each year since. The 1995 winners were Tomas Abrahamsson and Mike Kidd driving a Ford Escort Cosworth.

Finisher's plaque for the RSAC's Diamond Jubilee Scottish Rally in 1959.
© Alan Carlaw

1910 Rolls-Royce 40/50hp Shooting Brake in the 1960 RSAC Veteran Run at Bearsden. A good example of the famous "Silver Ghost" which originally belonged to the Duke of Windsor when Prince of Wales.
Photo courtesy Stuart Parker

Jimmy McInnes and Stuart Parker in a Mini Cooper 'S' on a Special Stage on the 1966 International Scottish Rally.
Photo courtesy Arlene McInnes

1979
"We want to create an image of dynamism, youth, style and driving pleasure," said Scotsman George Turnbull, Talbot chief, the newly-named former Chrysler Europe

Scottish Motor Museums

It is a matter of frustration in Scotland that the inventive genius of its people, which brought such benefit to the wider world, is so sparsely reflected in the industry of the homeland.

A nation renowned for its engineers and shipbuilders, for example, is left with little to show for the exquisite talents which could produce such masterpieces as the great Queens of Cunard.

But at least that heritage is preserved in the country's transport museums, reminding new generations of their forefathers' achievements and perhaps inspiring them towards triumphs of their own.

They range from the extensive Glasgow Transport Museum to the splendid collection of vintage and classic cars at Doune in Perthshire and the treasure of transport history at Alford in Grampian, which includes the Craigievar Express.

THE MUSEUM OF TRANSPORT, GLASGOW

The Glasgow museum covers everything from trains, trams and trolleys to ships, subways and of course motor cars, in the building of which Scotland at least made a promising start.

This Museum of Transport was housed in the old corporation tramway works at Albert Drive, Glasgow, between 1964 and 1987, by which time it was no longer adequate. With the building of the new Scottish Exhibition and Conference Centre at the former Queen's Dock,

Part of Glasgow's collection is this 1925 Austin 7
© Glasgow Museums

General view of some exhibits within the Museum of Transport, Glasgow
© Glasgow Museums

however, there would be a new role for the great Kelvin Hall, which had served the city well as a venue for exhibitions, concerts, circuses and sporting events.

Among other things taken over by the SECC was the Scottish Motor Show but now the Kelvin Hall would take on the dual purpose of a major indoor sports complex - and the new home of the transport museum.

Given that early foray into motor manufacture, there is naturally an excellent array of Scottish-built cars, like the Argylls, the Albions and the Arrol-Johnstons, coming right through to the Hillman Imp which brought mass production of the popular car to Linwood in the 1960s.

The individual genius of the Scottish engineer can be seen in the Robertson V4 two-stroke engine designed by James Robertson of Drymen, and in one of the famous Anderson Specials, built by James Anderson of Newton Mearns in the 1920s.

But the models are not all Scottish. You find such magnificent classic cars as the Rolls-Royce Phantom II of

There are doubtless a number of people in Glasgow who are living in houses not possessing the facilities for accommodation of a motor car and who would consider the purchase of a car had they such facilities. There must be a number of these prospective motorists in the West end of Glasgow alone and with a view to catering for them Mr Alexander Kennedy of laundry fame has established one of the completest garages it has been our pleasure to see. The building was not taken over and turned into a garage but was erected solely for the purpose of storing and repairing motor cars. It is absolutely fireproof, the only wood in the premises being in the window sashes and the vehicles themselves. The name of the firm is Botanic Gardens Motor Garage.
Motor World - 6 February 1908

Motor World - 2 June 1906
1980
The Metro was British Leyland's great white hope while the front-wheel drive Escort was a vital car for Ford.
The four-wheel-drive turbocharged Quattro was hailed as the greatest advance in car design during 1980.

One of the finest exhibits in the Glasgow Museum is this 23 hp Schneider which was used as a French Army Staff Car in WWI
© Glasgow Museums

1950 Central SMT Guy Arab Mk.III with Guy bodywork from the Vintage Bus Museum
© Keith A Gascoine

1957 Glasgow Corporation Daimler with Alexander bodywork now part of the Vintage Bus Museum
© Keith A Gascoine

1931, which was a gift from his wife to Sir William Burrell, the shipowner who gave his famous Burrell Collection to Glasgow.

So the exhibits range from the Model 'T' Ford to a beautiful Bentley Sedanca Coupe, an 1898 Benz Comfortable and a Lagonda Tourer to the popular Volkswagen Beetle and even Sir Clive Sinclair's short-lived C5 battery-powered tricycle.

In the commercial section there is a Ruston and Hornsby traction engine from 1920, an Albion butcher's van of 1910 and the first BMC lorry to be made at Bathgate in 1962.

THE SCOTTISH VINTAGE BUS MUSEUM

Glasgow also touches on the story of its corporation buses. But for the Scottish Vintage Bus Museum you travel to Lathalmond, on the outskirts of Dunfermline, to a former Ministry of Defence site once linked to the nearby Rosyth Naval Base.

And there you find a museum which recreates the authentic atmosphere of an old-time bus garage. Facing into the central aisle is a fascinating array of vintage buses in various states of re-building. There is a fleet of former Glasgow Corporation buses and an Edinburgh shed which houses the exhibits of the Lothian Bus Club.

There is an impressive turn-out of Leylands, Daimlers, Bedfords and Albions, several of which have been seen in television films requiring the atmosphere of a bygone day.

DOUNE MOTOR MUSEUM

The Earl of Moray (he was then Lord Doune) had no thoughts of starting a museum when he saw a 1934 Hispano-Suiza advertised in 1953. It was a time when exotic cars were still inexpensive to buy so he acquired it for his own use, little knowing it would become the first exhibit in the Doune Motor Museum, just north of Stirling.

It was 1961 before he added the Invicta and the Abbot Bentley to his private gathering of cars and a year later his growing interest in hill-climb competition landed him the SS

1981
British Leyland's Honda tie-up was consummated with the launch of the Triumph Acclaim, a rebadged Honda Ballade. Citroen produced 300 yellow 2CVs with bullet-hole stickers after a starring role in the James Bond movie "For Your Eyes Only"

1924 Hispano-Suiza 37.2hp Tourer from the Doune Collection
Photo courtesy Doune Motor Museum

Exhibits within the Grampian Transport Museum
© Grampian Transport Museum

*Doune's 1935 Rolls-Royce 40/50
Phantom II Continental*
Photo courtesy Doune Motor Museum

100 Jaguar and an 8 CM Maserati.

But his cars were needing to be housed in properly heated conditions and gradually the idea of a museum took shape. It was opened in 1970 and simply represents a personal choice of attractive cars from 1905 till 1968.

The 50 exhibits include the second oldest Rolls-Royce in the world and the Continental R-type Bentley which was presented to Stephen Hendry when he won the Embassy World Snooker tournament in 1994.

GRAMPIAN TRANSPORT MUSEUM

Scotland's car museums are neatly spread out across the land, with the Grampian one at the village of Alford in Aberdeenshire, well established as a popular tourist attraction in the north-east.

It was first suggested in the early 1970s when local enthusiasts sensed a growing interest in historic transport. Out of a public meeting in 1978 came the Grampian Transport Museum Association which would work towards a permanent exhibition.

The remains of the railway station at Alford became available and, with help from Grampian Region and some European funding, an exhibition hall was built and the museum opened in 1983.

A prime feature is the famous Craigievar Express, the first steam motor car seen in the North-east and the invention of a local postman, Andrew Lawson, who was another of those worthies with a rare talent for the mechanical.

He was alleged to have used it occasionally on his rounds though it caused much alarm and perhaps indignation among the horses of the district. Postie Lawson, who died in 1938, first drove his invention around 1897 and would have been intrigued to know that his Craigievar Express was such a celebrity 100 years later. It took part in the London-Brighton road race in 1971 without any difficulty.

Another attraction at Alford is the Birkhall, a Marshall portable steam engine given to Grampian by the Duke of Edinburgh from the royal estate at Balmoral. The old engine was used at a saw-mill on the Balmoral estate, powering it until its closure in the 1970s.

The outbreak of the First World War in September 1914 is certainly well covered in the magazine with comments on how this will affect the motor trade. Conversion of motor cars into ambulances with the British Red Cross Society appealing to all Scottish motorists on behalf of the transport work. In the following edition it goes on to report that there has been a generous response to the transport fund but further effort is urgently needed.
Motor World - 11 June 1914

1982
*A sad year in the world of Motor Sport. Colin Chapman, the founder of Lotus, died in December and Gilles Villeneuve was killed in practice in the Belgian Grand Prix.
Mark Thatcher went missing in the Sahara desert while taking part in the Paris to Dakar Rally.*

MYRETON MOTOR MUSEUM, ABERLADY

Well down the east coast, at Aberlady on the Firth of Forth, the Myreton Motor Museum has been amassing an impressive collection since 1966, including cars, commercials and military vehicles from the Second World War. Once again, you find

1927 Darracq DTS 15/40 from the Myreton collection. Coachbuilder was Gordon England for Sir Francis Samuelson.
Photo courtesy Myreton Motor Museum

A 1923 Hillman Sports 10.4hp. A rare survivor of the model made famous by Raymond Mays.
Photo courtesy Myreton Motor Museum

American General Electric buggy of 1899 vintage from the Myreton collection
Photo courtesy Myreton Motor Museum

them turning up in films.

There is a 1943 Hillman Light Utility military vehicle quite rare today. Myreton also has a 1925 Morris Commercial Type SW Series 1, among the very earliest commercials built by Morris.

Of special interest is the 1940 Renault Cabriolet, one of the last cars shipped out of France before the German occupation. At Myreton you find a 1923 Hillman Sports, made famous by Raymond Mays, the international race-car driver. And there is the 1935 Singer 972cc which raced successfully at Ards, Donnington, Brooklands and Le Mans

The oldest car in the museum is an 1896 Leon Bolle once owned by no less a figure than C S Rolls himself.

Sheriff Umpherston at Dunfermline in a collision case said that he learned to pay no attention to what an ordinary member of the public thought was the rate at which a motor car was travelling because he judged mainly by the noise it was making and he had no idea of speed. Will other Sheriffs please copy!
Motor World - December 1923

1983
Wearing seatbelts became compulsory in Great Britain and there was an immediate 20% drop in deaths and serious injuries in road accidents

MacBrayne for the Highlands

The name of MacBrayne is forever bound up with the romance of the Western Highlands and Islands, mainly through its steamers but also its buses.

David MacBrayne, who was born in 1814, was a nephew of G and J Burns, the well-known shipping people, and he in turn became synonymous with the steamers which plied the western waters of Scotland.

The company became a private limited one in 1906 and that was when it started to operate a bus service, the sole vehicle running between Fort William and North Ballachulish.

That was a German Daimler seating 35 people, bought second-hand from the Isle of Wight. The first new bus was a chain-driven 14-seater from the Albion works in Glasgow, bought in 1907.

David MacBrayne died in that same year, when he was 93. But his bus service continued to expand, taking on the Inverness-Glenurquhart route in 1911 because an opposition bus service was competing with the company's mail steamer on Loch Ness. Other would-be opposition

One of MacBrayne's original buses – an Albion which was delivered in 1907, the year of the death of David MacBrayne senior. It ran between Fort William and North Ballachulish which was MacBrayne's first bus route.

Photo courtesy Robert Grieves

MacBrayne's famous steamer King George V approaches Fort William pier during the summer of 1951, while three Maudslay coaches await to take the passengers on tour. Today, of course, there is no such facility available as the Oban to Fort William steamer service has long-since been abandoned.

Photo courtesy Robert Grieves

1984
Nissan finally agreed terms to build a factory in the UK at Sunderland and Honda also announced its plans for a plant at Swindon.

was bought out in 1938 and 1945.

MacBrayne had around 112 buses in the early 1950s, a prosperous time in the aftermath of the war when motor cars were scarce and people depended more on the bus.

The MacBrayne name disappeared from the bus routes in 1971 with the re-organisation which brought in the Scottish Bus Group. Some of the buses were preserved by individual enthusiasts.

But nothing stands still for long and the government policy of de-regulation has since put many bus services back into private ownership.

A small Bedford bus splashes its way from Carrick Castle to Lochgoilhead in the mid-60s – typical of the uneconomic rural services provided by MacBrayne's buses in the West Highlands and Islands
Photo courtesy Robert Grieves

The part that MacBrayne played in the life of the Western Isles is often illustrated in the following delightful anonymous verse:

The earth unto the Lord belongs
And all that it contains
Except, of course the Western Isles
And these are all MacBraynes.

An AEC coach awaits passengers and goods from the Mail Steamer Loch Fyne at Tarbert pier in 1966 before departing on the afternoon service to Glasgow
Photo courtesy Robert Grieves

Three men on a Scott scaled the Rest
Was quite a formidable test
They used Wakefield oil
To keep off the boil
And terrors of the Rest all went West.

A merry young maid of Braemar
Went out for a run on a Star
She let in the clutch
The smoothness was such
She ordered one more for Papa.

A guidy old guy from Milngavie
Bought a two-seater 8-cylinder Gavie
It took him so fast
When his breath came at last
All he could say was "Old Mavie."
Motor world - February 1922

1985
The Sinclair C5 was launched amid a flurry of publicity, but safety scares and woeful sales killed it off before the year was out.
Austin-Rover firmed up its ties with Honda.

Motoring Motivators

HENRY WALLACE

A 50-year-old Scot became head of the Japanese car-making empire Mazda in 1996..

Born in Edinburgh, Henry Wallace took over at the company's Hiroshima base, in a move designed to consolidate the growing ties between Mazda and Ford.

Henry Wallace was educated in Edinburgh and after taking an economics degree at Leicester University was recruited by Ford's financial management department in 1971.

Rising very quickly through the executive ranks Wallace soon saw himself as head of the Ford operations in Mexico and Venezuela before being seconded to Mazda in 1994 after the US firm took a 25% share in the Mazda company.

Past colleagues have described Henry Wallace as a "good guy to work for: very polished, very smart, aggressive but not imperious. He is a quietly intelligent Scotsman".

GEORGE TURNBULL

Scots born George Turnbull played an important part in many major motor industry operations and none more so than the giant South Korean conglomerate Hyundai. In 1972 they put him in charge of one of the biggest car factories in the world.

Turnbull had been second in command to Donald Stokes at British Leyland having charge of Austin-Morris as well as the truck and bus divisions before resigning and moving east.

After his successful spell with Hyundai, Turnbull moved to Iran to run the Paykan operation which assembled Hillman Hunters under licence. After the fall of the Shah he moved back to the UK to take over the reins at Peugeot Talbot Ltd which had absorbed the former Chrysler business.

Problems however with the ill-fated Rootes factory at Linwood saw Turnbull make his final move to Inchcape when he was given a knighthood and where he was still working at the time of his death.

It wasn't just his boardroom colleagues who felt the impact of this tough Scot. Many an opponent on the rugby field will testify about his will to win as a player with London Scottish.

Once described by Brian Llewelyn, then Puegeot Talbot's Public Relations Director, as "the best man-manager I've ever worked with and the greatest motivator".

IAN McALLISTER

Ian G McAllister, CBE, was appointed Chairman of Ford of Britain in December 1991, having previously been Managing Director of the Company from September 1991.

He was born in Glasgow in 1943 and graduated from London University, where he gained a BSc in Economics in 1964 when he joined Ford.

He held various positions and in 1980 he was appointed Director, Parts Sales, for Ford of Britain. In 1981 he moved to Germany as Director, Product and Marketing, in Ford of Europe's Parts Operations.

Mr McAllister is a member of the Executive Committee and Council of the Society of Motor Manufacturers and Traders; a member of the President's Committee of the Confederation of British Industry; a Vice President of both the Institute of the Motor Industry and the Motor and Allied Trades Benevolent Fund; and a Companion of the British Institute of Management.

He is also a Fellow of the Royal Society of Arts; a Board member of Anglia University; a Trustee of the Beaulieu National Motor Museum; and a member of the Lord's Taverners.

Mr McAllister was awarded the CBE in the Queen's New Year Honours in 1996..

Sir George Turnbull
The Herald

Ian McAllister
© Ford Motor Company

1986
Wheel clamping was introduced in London to curb traffic in the capital.

Doonhamer Designers

What does Noblehill Primary School in Dumfries have in common with the sleek sophisticated design of some of the most advanced cars in the world today? The answer of course is that the school was the first stepping stone to success for the brilliant young Scottish car designers Ian and Moray Callum, whose proud mother Sheila still lives in Dumfries.

Ian, the elder made his way via Dumfries Academy, Morrisons Academy Crieff, Glasgow School of Art and Royal College of Art in London where he received a Masters degree in Automotive Design before joining Ford and ending up as Ghia Design Manager in Turin. From Italy it was then back to Britain where he was invited to join the Oxfordshire based TWR Design as Chief Designer to prepare the shape of the new Volvo Coupé and convertible scheduled for launch in 1997.

Moray, four years younger than Ian, shared his brother's passion for the motor car and after Dumfries Academy, Heriot Watt University and Napier College graduated with a BA in Industrial Design. It was sponsorship however from Chrysler UK that saw Moray follow in his brothers footsteps and receive his Masters degree in Automotive Design from the Royal College of Art in London.

After a time with Puegeot in Coventry and Paris, Moray moved to Ford at the Ghia studio in Turin before taking up the post as Design Manager of the Ford 'large car' studio in Detroit USA.

Ironically on the same day as Ian's Aston Martin DB7 was launched at the Geneva Motor Show in 1993, the Lagonda Vignale designed by Moray was also revealed.

Lagonda production had petered out in 1989 and it was then that Moray Callum, working in the Ghia studio in Turin, was given the opportunity to style the brand new Lagonda Vignale.

By coincidence, another Scottish connection with Lagonda was that the original company was founded by Wilbur Gunn, an American descended from the North-East of Scotland. Lagonda was a small village on Buck Creek near Springfield,

Moray and Ian Callum pictured together at the 1993 Geneva Motor Show.
At the show Ian was awarded the Jim Clark Memorial Award for his design work on the Aston Martin
DB7 and the Lagonda Vignale designed by Moray was also revealed.
Photo courtesy of Sheila Callum

Ohio where Gunn grew up.

Ian and Moray Callum – "Doonhamers from Dumfries" – designers extraordinary!

The Car with One Door

When the famous Sword collection was auctioned off at Balgray Farm near Irvine, an anonymous member of the RSAC made a successful bid for the superb 1922 15.9hp Arrol-Johnston registered DL 2560.

Although the car remains in the RSAC's ownership it is permanently based at the home of the famed Scottish coachbuilders, Penman Engineering of Dumfries, which completely restored the car just before the Dumfries Octocentenary celebrations in 1986. Indeed Penman's still manufacture specialist vehicle bodies a mere half-mile from the original Arrol-Johnston factory at Heathhall.

Current Managing Director of Penman's, Edwin Hunter, often takes his turn at the wheel of this magnificent car (the 15.9 being one of the most successful cars ever built by Arrol-Johnston) but Ian Gray, a supervisor at Penman's, is its most regular driver, notching almost 1500 miles each summer in the car when it takes part in events all over Scotland.

Enthusiasts stare in wonder at the body of this remarkable car because it does indeed have only one door; (on the front passenger's side). The spare wheel is mounted where the driver's door would normally be!

Ian Gray estimates that the car's top speed with its 2613cc engine is about 38mph. He even boasts of climbing up over the Devil's Beef Tub on the A701 in top gear!

After DL2560 comes off the road at the end of each summer, it stays under wraps at Penmans over the following winter before emerging in the spring each year, raring to go and once again demonstrating the quality of Arrol-Johnston engineering and craftsmanship.

![The beautifully restored 1922 15.9hp Arrol-Johnston in the Dumfries countryside]

The beautifully restored 1922 15.9hp Arrol-Johnston in the Dumfries countryside
Photo courtesy Ian Gray

DL2560 with regular driver Ian Gray (Penman Engineering Supervisor) and Marcel Pullinger (son of the legendary T C Pullinger) seen outside the former Arrol-Johnston works at Heathhall, Dumfries.
Photo courtesy Ian Gray

Taxicabs for Glasgow and Edinburgh. The Magistrates Committee of Glasgow considered an application on Tuesday last from a London firm requesting permission to run fifty taximeter cabs in Glasgow. The applicants proposed to send one of the taxis for inspection and approval and the Magistrates agreed to examine the vehicle before pronouncing on the application. A similar application has been considered by the Edinburgh Town Council.
Motor World - 28 December 1907

Quite a sensation caused in Glasgow recently by Sheriff Blair in admonishing a total of fifty motorists who appeared before him on speed charges, as a recognition of the public services they performed as motorists during the recent General Strike. This is a revolution in itself!
Motor World - May 1926

1988
British Aerospace bought Rover, helped significantly by the Government's controversial sweetener (later to cause a political row) which wrote off debts.

Monte Carlo or Bust!

It was a wintry January of 1911 that heralded the birth of the now famous Monte Carlo Rally. The underlying scheme was the basis of all succeeding Rallies. Competitors could start from various cities in Europe in such a way as to hold a minimum average of 10mph to Monte Carlo, checking in at various cities and towns en route. Average speed, distance covered, number of passengers, comfort and mechanical state at the finish gained marks which decided the winner of 10,000 francs and the Rally.

In 1924, a year in which even motor-cycles were included, the Rally was won by the daring driver J Ledure who was the only entrant who actually started from Glasgow driving a Bignan.

The year 1926 was however a milestone in Scottish motoring history as it marked the first-ever British winner of the Rally from the most unlikely starting point of John O'Groats in the North of Scotland. The driver was the Hon Victor Bruce, who won easily in his AC partnered by W J Brunnell, at the same time picking up the 2-litre class in the hill climb.

Bruce had persuaded the organisers to make John O'Groats the British starting point.

In 1927, Bruce and his wife, the former Mildred Mary Petre, started once again from John O'Groats in a Weymann-bodied AC sports saloon. At first glance Mrs Bruce looked as if she was there in a purely ornamental role, as she posed at the starting line with her fashionable hat, fur-collared coat, silk stockings and a string of pearls. Nothing however could have been further from the truth as this lady driver extraordinary won the Coupe des Dames, was sixth in the overall Rally and first in the 2-litre class on the Mont des Mules. Not bad considering she drove the full 1529 miles to Monte Carlo battling with snow, fog and icy roads for 70 hours and 20 minutes.

Quite a lady was the Hon Mrs Victor Bruce as she went on to set up records not only on the road, but in the air and on water: first solo flight England-to-Japan, first crossing of the Yellow Sea, first prize in show jumping at Royal Windsor in 1939 and Order of the Million Elephants and White Umbrella (French Indo-China).

It was however the Bruces' efforts that firmly put the remote Scottish outpost of John O'Groats on the Rally starting map for many years to come. People who saw a car with the special Monte Carlo plates realised what was happening and felt the romance of that long joyous trip.

Sadly as British entries for the famous Rally dwindled over the years the romantic starting point of John O'Groats as well as Glasgow could no longer be sustained

The Hon Mrs Victor Bruce, not to be outdone by her husband, won the Coupe des Dames in this AC saloon in 1927. Here the car is being checked by Rally officials.

Congratulations to A K Stevenson, Secretary of the RSAC on his inclusion in the New Year Honours List. His OBE has been well earned for apart from his connection with the RSAC since 1904 he has been Chief Transport Officer of the Scottish Red Cross transport of wounded department of two wars. During this last war he has operated 480 vehicles scattered over Scotland and his staff drove over 8 million miles and carried more than 1.2 million patients. Mr Stevenson was also the organiser of the Glasgow Special Constabulary Mobile Section, formed at the time of the General Strike. There is no one in Scotland today who knows more about Scottish motoring than A K Stevenson and he has always taken a keen interest in the sporting side also. His circle of friends is wide and there will be much gratification that his good work has been recognised.
Motor World - January 1946

1989

In the face of declining profits, Jaguar was courted by Ford and General Motors, much against its wishes, but the government waived its golden share and Ford bought the company.

The Scots–American Connection

DAVID BUICK

From the East of Scotland came two of the most prominent figures ever to have graced the vast American motor car industry.

Born in Arbroath, David Dunbar Buick emigrated to America with his parents in 1857 and eventually gave his name to the car on which the giant General Motors empire in Detroit was founded.

The young Buick began work in America as a plumber. Indeed few people know today that David Buick was the inventor of the white porcelain bath.

Always tinkering with engines in his workshop however, Buick built his first car in 1903 and the first production model the following year, heralding the birth of the Buick Motor Company which in a mere two years was worth $1,500,000. Buick cars were also the first to be equipped with windshields and valve-in-head engines.

After withdrawing from the motor business, Buick had the misfortune to become involved with an oil venture in California and land deals during a Florida boom, both of which were largely unsuccessful, resulting in serious financial reverses.

David Dunbar Buick eventually died of cancer aged 74 on 5 March 1929, survived by his second wife Margaret, two sons and two daughters. At the time of his death he was a clerk in an industrial trade school and almost destitute. But he left behind his memorial – a car which remained in the forefront of American automotive engineering through the succeeding decades and was famous all over the world. A true "Red Lichtie" and one of Scotland's most famous sons!

David Buick is commemorated in his birthplace Arbroath in 1994. Helping to dedicate a plaque are Eric Buick of Arbroath(no relation), Robert E Coletta, Lawrence R Gustin (both of Buick) and Provost Brian Milne of Angus District
Courtesy Buick Motor Division

ALEXANDER WINTON

On April Fool's Day 1898 the first automobile ever commercially sold in America was dispatched by a Scotsman, Alexander Winton, from his small factory in Cleveland, Ohio. The car cost $1,000.

Born on 20 June 1860 in Grangemouth, where his father Alex manufactured agricultural implements, the young Winton made model steamboats and sailed them on the Forth near his home. He went to sea from Glasgow on the Atlantic steamers, eventually landing a job in a New York iron works.

The brilliant young Scottish engineer and inventor rapidly graduated from making his own bicycles to establishing the vast Winton Motor Carriage Co of Cleveland, Ohio. Although Alexander Winton did not claim that he made the first car in America there seems no doubt that he was the first to make it commercially.

Winton's racing car "Bullet No.1" established a record of a mile in 52.2 seconds in 1902 at Daytona Beach, the first time that the beach was used for racing. In 1903 the "Bullet No 2", which was driven by the American racing driver Barney Oldfield, set new world records for 5 miles and 10 miles at the Empire City track.

The Industrial Vehicle Parade held in Glasgow last week under the auspices of the SAC demonstrated the growing popularity of the self-propelled vehicle in the commercial and industrial world, a popularity daily manifest from the number and variety of motor vans to be seen traversing the city's busiest thoroughfares. One of the most thoroughgoing displacements of horse-drawn vans was carried through about two years ago by the proprietors of the Glasgow News. A pioneer in many ways, the News was the first daily journal in Great Britain to make the transition from horse haulage to automobilism at one stride.
Motor World - 15 October 1908

1990
Nigel Mansell announced his retirement but then promptly accepted a drive for Williams in 1991.
The Mini Cooper was revived and almost immediately took half of all Mini sales.

"That Car Ahead is a Winton" – the 1904 model was the season's distinctive hit in America with foremost international engineers uniting in praise of its genuine merit. American journalists said – "It's success is as certain as the downcurrent of the Mississippi in flood times"!

Courtesy Robert Stormont, Illinois

Never forgetting his love of Scotland and the great yachts being built in the land of his birth, Winton negotiated with Cox & Stevens, the New York naval architects, to design a motor yacht second to none on the Great Lakes. Named *La Belle* after his Paisley-born wife, the yacht was indeed one of the most luxurious ever built.

Alexander Winton, who died on 21 June 1932 in Cleveland, was a courageous pioneer, doing much to establish the motor car in America.

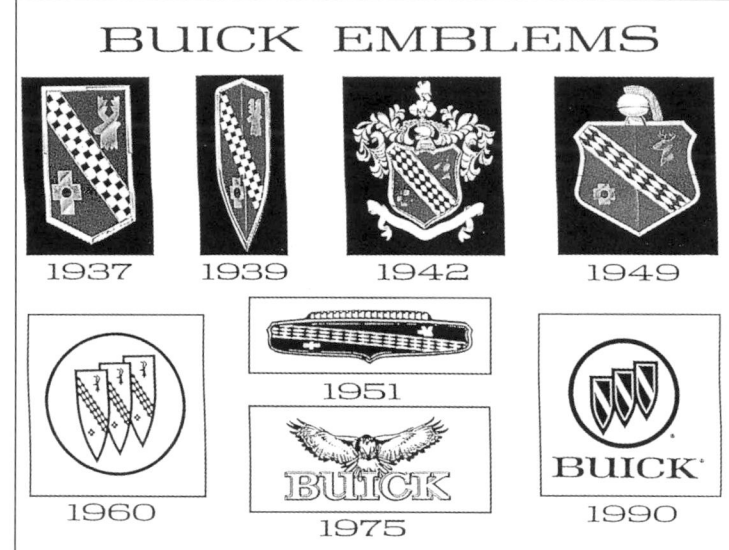

Buick Motor Division first used the Buick family crest on its 1937 models.

In 1959, the logo underwent a major revision. The tri-shield was introduced to represent the three Buick models then being built. All of the original crest symbols and colours were retained, with the major difference being that instead of one shield, there were now the three overlapping shields in red, white and blue.

In 1975 the Buick Hawk concept was initiated. It was so well received that the symbol of a hawk perched on block letters of Buick was expanded to all car lines. In 1976, though the tri-shield was retained as Buick's primary mark. The hawk soared to popularity and a red-tailed hawk named -"Happy" was even trained to land on Buick hood ornaments in television ads.

The Buick family crest, like the Buick nameplate, keeps alive the memory of David Dunbar Buick, who started a chain of events that gave birth to Buick Motor Co. and led to the creation of General Motors – the world's largest automaker.

Oliver and Sword – Collectors Supreme

GEORGE OLIVER

Thanks to the dedicated efforts of two Scots, cars and records relating to Scotland's Motoring history have been safeguarded by the Museum of Transport in Glasgow and willingly made available for motoring researchers. .

The precious George A Oliver Collection of motoring history in Scotland covers almost 30 years of zealous research and technical history.

George Oliver was a man of many talents who served in the RAF and was later employed by the Design Council. It was, however, his life-long interest in motoring matters, coupled with his exceptional memory for which he will be best remembered.

Apart from being a first class photographer, George was an outstanding illustrator of the motor car and the author of several motoring books.

George Oliver was also a Rolls-Royce enthusiast, symbolising his life-long pursuit of quality.

JOHN C SWORD

In September 1962, a unique event took place at Balgray Farm near Irvine where motoring enthusiasts from America, Britain and Europe gathered for an auction of over 100 vintage cars which realised £50,000.

The cars were just part of the incredible collection of veteran and vintage vehicles which was once the pride and joy of the late John C Sword, a remarkable man who had successfully managed various forms of transport during a colourful career.

The son of a baker in Airdrie, young Sword worked as a vanman before serving in the Royal Flying Corps during the 1914-18 war. That was when he became intrigued by motoring and aviation, realising that cars and aeroplanes would revolutionise transportation.

In the early 1920's, Sword began a service of four buses between Coatbridge and Kilsyth which eventually expanded into a fleet of 400 operating all over the West of Scotland and to England. He was also a pioneer of air travel in Scotland and at one time owned 26 aircraft as well as starting the first air ferry and air ambulance service to the Western Isles.

In a collection which once stretched to more than 200 at Balgray Farm, Sword had a weakness for cars associated with famous people, like Nurse Cavell's two-seater 1906 Rover, Sylvia Parkhurst's 1910 Standard, Lord Catto's 1912 Rover, the famous leather-winged Rolls-Royce owned by the Duke of Buccleuch, the remarkable 1926 Hispano-Suiza "Chitty Chitty Bang" owned by Count Sabrowski and a post-war armour plated Rolls-Royce Silver Wraith built for Eva Peron.

John Sword was a shrewd, down-to-earth character who never forgot his vanman's days in Airdrie. His pawky sense of humour was never more clearly illustrated than when he was entertaining guests aboard a splendid yacht. Among them was a very important eastern gentleman who had an unpronounceable name, but John solved the problem by saying in his broad Airdrie accent, 'We'll just all cry him Cherlie!"

John Cuthill Sword--a remarkable Scotsman who must rank as the most insatiable collector of the 20th century.

At the Balgray Auction, A S E Browning, former Curator of Technology, Glasgow Museums said............

"Old cars are like old people. Some smoke a little, some drink a little, some are not very strong. Some have stiffness at the joints and others have lost their youthful complexions. Some need to be cared for and given a good home. All, however, have developed character and much can be learned from them. They are good company."

George A Oliver
Photo courtesy of Cordelia Oliver

John Cuthill Sword
© Glasgow Museums

1992
*Gatso speed cameras flashed for the first time in Britain.
A new 20-group insurance system put most premiums up, but GTi drivers were hit hardest!*

Motoring Miscellany

A welcome sight for stranded motorists was the 'AA Man' on his motor cycle combination. He would offer a military salute to passing cars displaying the AA badge although it is often said that no salute indicated a speed trap ahead! Land Rovers, like mini garages, were used in the remoter areas of Scotland. The roadside telephone boxes, for which members had keys, provided a means of communication.

© Alan Carlaw (2)
© Automobile Association

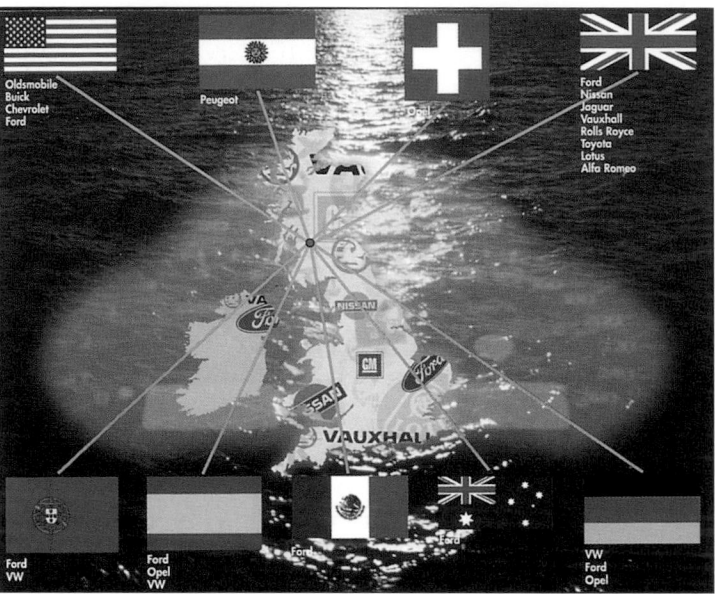

McGavigan's International Markets and products

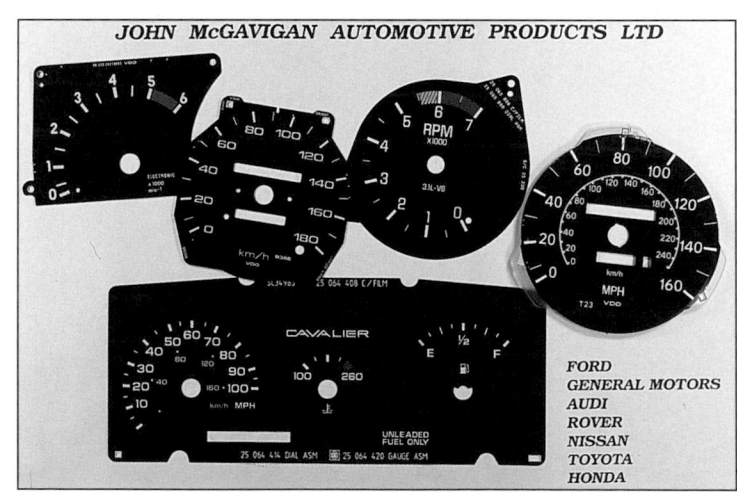

JOHN McGAVIGAN

Not much may have survived from the early promise of Scotland's car industry but the firm of John McGavigan from Kirkintilloch, near Glasgow, is a shining exception.

The firm was established in 1860 and now enjoys a worldwide market from its manufacture of appliances for the motor industry.

The kind of product which emerges from the McGavigan plant includes dials, gauges, plastic overlays and a wide range of instruments which are floodlit, backlit or "secret-till-lit".

More than 100,000 components are despatched every day, across Britain, Europe, the United States and beyond, proving that Scotland has far from lost its grip on the automotive industry.

1993
This was a big year for Vauxhall with the new Corsa and Omega, helping to knock Ford off the Number One spot in August.

Two Albion City of Glasgow Police Vans. One of these "Black Marias" was used to transport mass murderer Peter Manuel on his last journey to the gallows. It was later used as a fruit and veg van in Maryhill!

© Albion Archive, Biggar

The Scottish Motor Industry was briefly revived when in October 1983 the Duke of Argyll launched the new Argyll Turbo Car from his home at Inveraray Castle. The Turbo GT which was built by Argyll Turbo Cars of Lochgilphead with finish and trim by Avon Coachworks of Warwick was described as a car of vision, design skill and engineering realisation; a car of performance and technical excellence but above all – a car for the discerning driver. Sadly, the car was not a success and production ceased.

The Glasgow motorist is so apt to congratulate himself on the complacent and sympathetic attitude of the authorities towards the self propelled vehicle that he is in danger of forgetting that there is another side to the question. Anyone who has driven in Glasgow knows the utter disregard of the simplest decencies of the road of the average lorry driver. The pedestrian who has so aptly been termed the "chartered libertine of the highway" is although above rules and regulations apparently in the second city, a graver danger to himself and to the motorist than in the majority of the big cities either in Scotland or England. Motorists who have not much experience of traffic driving in other towns may think that conditions are much the same everywhere but their minds are rapidly abused if they enter into conversation on the subject with a visitor.
Motor World - 16 February 1907

1994
The Probe coupé became the first American-built Ford to be sold in the UK for 70 years.
Ayrton Senna and Roland Ratzenberger both died in high speed crashes at Imola.

1928 Albion Merryweather Fire Appliance
Galway Fire Brigade
© Glasgow Museums

Logan Morrison leads a trio of Imps
on the Ingliston Circuit in the early 1970s
Courtesy Logan Morrison

The driver and navigator positions in a Mini-Cooper.
Note that the speedometer is located in front of the navigator.
Courtesy Logan Morrison

Motor Fuel Ration Book and coupons

Richard Noble OBE

Fastest man on four wheels!

Thrust 2, driven by Edinburgh born Richard Noble OBE, gained for Great Britain the World Land Speed Record on the 4th of October 1983 at a speed of 633.468 mph. Designed by John Ackroyd and powered by a Rolls-Royce Avon 302 engine from a British Aerospace Lightning aircraft, *Thrust 2* achieved the record at Black Rock Desert in Nevada, USA. The successful attempt on the record was the result of long planning – nine years – dedicated effort by a small team of specialist enthusiasts and support from a number of British companies.

The highest land speed attained in Britain is 263.92 mph also by Richard Noble in *Thrust 2* at Greenham Common, Berks on 25 September 1980

© Chris Rock

First British Truck Racing Champion was Heather Baillie in 1990

First Scotsman to be Stock Car World Champion (Formula Two) was Jimmy Wallace in 1988/89

Britain's top motoring teacher in 1990 was Scotswoman Barbara Coverdale.

Finally where would the world of motoring be without tarmacadam roads invented by Scotsman John Loudon McAdam (1756-1836) or even the inventor of tar, Scotsman Archibald Cochrane (1749-1831).

1995
This was the year in which Formula 1 Number Two drivers made their presences felt – Schumacher's understudy Johnny Herbert won two races and Hill's team mate Scotsman David Coulthard one.

Scottish Registrations

The rapid increase of motor car ownership from the mid 1890's necessitated some form of vehicle identification and registration together with the licensing of their drivers. This was brought about by the Motor Car Act of 1903 which established the general principles for England and Wales with similar laws for Scotland and Ireland. Registration was entrusted to county and county borough councils in England and Ireland and counties and large burghs in Scotland. These authorities opened registers for motor cars and motor cycles where a fee of 20 shillings was payable for each motor car registered and 5 shillings for a motor cycle. The registration numbers were to be displayed on plates mounted vertically at the front and rear of vehicles and size and shape of plate were specified. The numbering system had to be capable of more or less infinite expansion so it was kept as simple as possible with each registration authority being allocated an index mark consisting of one or two letters (I and Q were omitted to avoid confusion with J and O).

Special arrangements were made to identify vehicles registered in Scotland where all marks were to include the letter G, S or V and Ireland was to use I and Z. By the early 1930's a number of authorities had exhausted the two letter, four figure system and the more familiar three figure, three letter marks were introduced. This system too reached its capacity and the letters were placed after the numbers. A suffix letter was added to the 6 digit marks in 1963, the additional digit indicating the year of registration. This initially changed on 1 January each year although it now takes effect from 1 August. After the letter Y was used from August 1982 the system was changed to use a prefix letter from August 1983. The local authority records were eventually transferred to a central agency when the DVLC was set up.

The vehicle marks issued to Scotland are listed below, although some of these were subsequently reallocated to other areas. The reissue of early registrations which had lapsed due to the original vehicle going out of use could be obtained by application to the authority concerned and the payment of the statutory search fee of 1 shilling. The increase in the desire for personalised numbers and the central licensing system has changed all this into a vast money making business - both by the DVLC and numerous private companies. Whereas it was originally quite straightforward to trace the original place of registration of a vehicle the issue of personalised marks and cherished numbers has rather muddied this principle.

Scottish Index Marks and registration authorities

AG	Ayrshire	SB	Argyllshire
AS	Nairnshire	SC	Edinburgh Burgh
AV	Aberdeenshire	SD	Ayrshire
BS	Orkney	SE	Banffshire
CS	Ayrshire	SF	Edinburgh Burgh
DS	Peeblesshire	SG	Edinburgh Burgh
ES	Perthshire	SH	Berwickshire
FS	Edinburgh Burgh	SJ	Bute
G	Glasgow Burgh	SK	Caithness-shire
GA	Glasgow Burgh	SL	Clackmannanshire
GB	Glasgow Burgh	SM	Dumfriesshire
GD	Glasgow Burgh	SN	Dunbartonshire
GE	Glasgow Burgh	SO	Morayshire
GG	Glasgow Burgh	SP	Fife
GM	Motherwell & Wishaw Burgh	SR	Angus
GS	Perthshire	SS	East Lothian
HS	Renfrewshire	ST	Inverness-shire
JS	Ross & Cromarty	SU	Kincardineshire
KS	Roxburghshire	SV	Kinross-shire
LS	Selkirkshire	SW	Kirkcudbrightshire
MS	Stirlingshire	SX	Linlithgow
NS	Sutherlandshire	SY	Midlothian
OS	Wigtownshire	TS	Dundee Burgh
PS	Shetland	US	Glasgow Burgh
RG	Aberdeen Burgh	V	Lanarkshire
RS	Aberdeen Burgh	VA	Lanarkshire
S	Edinburgh Burgh	VD	Lanarkshire
SA	Aberdeenshire	VS	Greenock
WG	Stirlingshire		
WS	Leith Burgh		
XS	Paisley Burgh		
YS	Glasgow Burgh		

The Registration of motor cars became compulsory in 1904 at which time the speed limit was raised from 12 to 20 mph. The premier Scottish number S 1 went to that great motoring enthusiast Sir J H A McDonald, the Lord Justice Clerk, who had been interested in horseless carriages since the mid-1890s and who later became Lord Kingsburgh. Some other registrations were as follows:-

DS 1 (Peebles) Sir D F Hay
G 1 (Glasgow) R J Smith
HS 1 (Renfrew) W Todd
KS 1 (Roxburgh) W Blair
LS 1 (Selkirk) Dr I B Ronaldson
RS 1 (Aberdeen) R S Jackson
S 1 (Edinburgh) Sir J H A McDonald
SA 1 (Aberdeenshire) D A Ramsay
SB 1 (Argyll) J S Matthew
SH 1 (Berwick) Sir G H Boswell
SJ 1 (Bute) The Rt Hon G A Murray
SR 1 (Forfar) A M White
SU 1 (Kincardinshire) A J Ogston
SY 1 (Midlothian) J A Maconochie
DS 1 (Dundee) A Watt
V 1 (Lanark) Capt H S Streatfield